Wild Mushrooms

by

Anne Pié

NEW YORK HOLLYWOOD LONDON TORONTO

SAMUELFRENCH.COM

Copyright © 1995, 2008 by Anne Pié

ALL RIGHTS RESERVED

CAUTION: Professionals and amateurs are hereby warned that *WILD MUSHROOMS* is subject to a royalty. It is fully protected under the copyright laws of the United States of America, the British Commonwealth, including Canada, and all other countries of the Copyright Union. All rights, including professional, amateur, motion picture, recitation, lecturing, public reading, radio broadcasting, television and the rights of translation into foreign languages are strictly reserved. In its present form the play is dedicated to the reading public only.

The amateur live stage performance rights to *WILD MUSHROOMS* are controlled exclusively by Samuel French, Inc., and royalty arrangements and licenses must be secured well in advance of presentation. PLEASE NOTE that amateur royalty fees are set upon application in accordance with your producing circumstances. When applying for a royalty quotation and license please give us the number of performances intended, dates of production, your seating capacity and admission fee. Royalties are payable one week before the opening performance of the play to Samuel French, Inc., at 45 W. 25th Street, New York, NY 10010.

Royalty of the required amount must be paid whether the play is presented for charity or gain and whether or not admission is charged.

Stock royalty quoted upon application to Samuel French, Inc.

For all other rights than those stipulated above, apply to: Samuel French, Inc., at 45 W. 25th Street, New York, NY 10010.

Particular emphasis is laid on the question of amateur or professional readings, permission and terms for which must be secured in writing from Samuel French, Inc.

Copying from this book in whole or in part is strictly forbidden by law, and the right of performance is not transferable.

Whenever the play is produced the following notice must appear on all programs, printing and advertising for the play: "Produced by special arrangement with Samuel French, Inc."

Due authorship credit must be given on all programs, printing and advertising for the play.

ISBN 978-0-573-66271-3   Printed in U.S.A.   #25643

No one shall commit or authorize any act or omission by which the copyright of, or the right to copyright, this play may be impaired.

No one shall make any changes in this play for the purpose of production.

Publication of this play does not imply availability for performance. Both amateurs and professionals considering a production are strongly advised in their own interests to apply to Samuel French, Inc., for written permission before starting rehearsals, advertising, or booking a theatre.

No part of this book may be reproduced, stored in a retrieval system, or transmitted in any form, by any means, now known or yet to be invented, including mechanical, electronic, photocopying, recording, videotaping, or otherwise, without the prior written permission of the publisher.

IMPORTANT BILLING AND CREDIT REQUIREMENTS

All producers of *WILD MUSHROOMS must* give credit to the Author of the Play in all programs distributed in connection with performances of the Play, and in all instances in which the title of the Play appears for the purposes of advertising, publicizing or otherwise exploiting the Play and/or a production. The name of the Author *must* appear on a separate line on which no other name appears, immediately following the title and *must* appear in size of type not less than fifty percent of the size of the title type.

WILD MUSHROOMS was given its West Coast premier by CRC Entertainment in association with George Siafaris on November 12, 2003 at The American Renegade Theatre in North Hollywood, CA. The production was directed by T. J. Castronovo and was produced by Michael J. Carazza, T. J. Castronovo, Tonje Larsgard and David Cox. The cast, crew and design team were as follows:

CAST:

Gabriel Bologna
Kate Forster
Robert Gallo
Kelley Grager
James Grimaldi
Les Hart
Micah Henson
John LaMotta
Chi Chi Navarro
Barbara Ross

SET - John M. Crowther
LIGHTING DESIGN - Luke Moyer
SOUND - Alberto Romano
COSTUMES - Ana Wilson
STAGE MANAGER - Stefanie Ibanez
PHOTOGRAPHER - Alberto Romano
PUBLICITY - Robert Axelrod/Marcia Groff
CASTING - Jean Scoccimarro

THE CAST

BENNY SCRIVENTE - Italian-looking; in his late forties or early fifties; overwhelmed with raising his uncooperative family

JOEY SCRIVENTE - Average-looking thirteen year old intelligent; smart-mouthed; feels neglected by all

DODIE - Attractive, naive, early twenties sweetly innocent

REGINA - Lovely, sensual, mid-twenties eager in her pursuit of many suitors

AUNT ROSE - Older than Benny; colorful, flamboyant; an eccentric and a true clairvoyant

EVIEL KHARREN - Attorney; ethnic and good-looking; business-like; late twenties, early thirties

MARIO - Early thirties; suave, slick; street savy

ANGELO PECORINO - Late forties, early fifties swaggering Mafiosa-type

THE DON - Small in stature; elderly but totally endearing in his dotage

SETTING

Act One
Dinner Time - The kitchen in the modest home of the Scrivente family

Act Two
Scene I - Same place - One o'clock the following Sunday afternoon

Scene II - Thirty minutes later

PLACE

The modest Bronx home of the BENNY SCRIVENTE family.

The setting is the kitchen of the house. The back door is stage right with a window in it with a valance at the top. The sink is directly to the left of the door with a window over it with a matching valance. If practical, stairs to Aunt Rose's apartment can be seen through the window, and she's is also seen descending them on her entrances.

Under the sink is a cupboard along with other kitchen cupboards. Various Italian products sit on an open shelf... cans of tomatoes, olive oil, etc. Also, a large bottle of Mylanta sits in a prominent spot. A small radio sits on the left of the counter as well as the telephone. A small dish of black olives sit on the front of the counter facing the table.

The refrigerator is on the back wall and the stove is directly to its left, behind a counter. In front of the counter are two bar stools. The kitchen table and chairs are stage right, behind which is a small china cabinet.

An open hallway is at the back wall, the stage right entrance to the front of the house and the dining room. The stage left entrance leads to the bathroom and bedrooms. On the stage-left inside kitchen wall is a light switch.
At curtain, Benny is stirring something in a pot. He also opens the oven door to check its contents. He is wearing the trousers and short-sleeved shirt of a postal employee, with a frilly half-apron around his waist. Joey is at the table editing lines in a notebook. His book-bag is on a corner of the table which is also strewn with paper and pens.

ACT ONE

(At curtain, Joey Scrivente is seated at the kitchen table with a notebook and pencil in front of him. His father, Benny, is preparing dinner at the stove as he listens to a newscast on the radio.)

NEWSCASTER. And now, for the news. The House Investigating Commission on Organized Crime Kingpins was caught by surprise today when suspected leaders of far-flung factions of the Bambino's "La Famiglia Segreto", or Secret Family, were seen slipping into the city allegedly to attend a birthday party in honor of its well-known Don, Sarlo Bambino. A tight-lipped, U.S. Attorney General Alfredo Tortellini, coordinator of the Commission, is shown here entering the downtown offices of the FBI. Meanwhile, in the world of sports, spring training began today in Winter Haven.

(Benny turns off the radio and chides Joey.)

BENNY. Joey! What's the heck is the matter with you? I said to clear the table and you're sittin' there like a statue!

JOEY. In a minute, Pop.

BENNY. How many times do I have to say it. Clear the table. Your sisters will be home from work any second.

JOEY. *(Lost in scribbling in his book)* In a minute, Pop.

BENNY. *(Checks the oven)* We're all going to sit down to a nice family dinner and I want everything to be just right. You know how important family dinners are in this house.

(Lifts the lid on pot and tastes from spoon. Nods his approval.)

JOEY. Family dinner. I know what that means. You all eat while I get picked on.

BENNY. *(Replaces pot lid with a clank)* Pick on this, *capo tosto*.... hard head! Did you hear me? Or am I talking to the wall? The *table*.

JOEY. Yeah, Pop. I heard. Clear it.

BENNY. And get out a good table cloth; the one your mother liked, with the little roses and pansies all over.

JOEY. She never used that one when we had anything with sauce.

BENNY. Then get the red-checkered one. That don't show.

(Sets dinner plates up on counter)

JOEY. But we'll have to wash and iron it.

BENNY. *(Shouts)* When is the last time I asked you to iron?

JOEY. Yesterday!

BENNY. I only suggested! And get the good wine glasses from the dining room.

JOEY. Can I have some wine, too?

BENNY. Why not? It's a special occasion. You can have a sip of mine.

JOEY. Big deal, a sip!

BENNY. Make a fuss, you won't get any at all!

JOEY. All right! Don't bite my head off.

(Pause, as he thinks)

Pop, what's another word for pregnant?

BENNY. *(Comes out from behind the counter)* What the heck are you writing?

JOEY. Uh.... a project.

BENNY. For school? They're making you write stuff about pregnant?

JOEY. It's for... uh... science class. Animals get pregnant, you know.

BENNY. If it's for school, look it up in the dictionary.

JOEY. I did. But saying "she was **gravid** with child" didn't sound right.

BENNY. *Gravid?* What the heck is gravid?

JOEY. Oh, Pop! It's another word for pregnant.

BENNY. Oh, yeah? Well, an animal wouldn't be gravid with *child*. It would be with a puppy... or a baby lion.

JOEY. *(Scornfully)* Pop, for your information, lions have *cubs*.

BENNY. *(Shouts) Excuse* me, Doctor I.Q. Cubs, then.

JOEY. Don't get bent out of shape. It's just an expression. *(Thinks)* How do you feel about "knocked?

BENNY. Will you look at the mouth on that kid! No "knocked!"

JOEY. It's descriptive.

BENNY. It's too descriptive. That's *out*. Got it?

JOEY. All right. It's *out*.

(Scratches it out of book with vehemence)

But you're suppressing my creativity.

BENNY. You wanna see *real* suppress. Just try using that kind of language around here again.

(To the ceiling)

Do you see what I have to contend with, Lenora? It's no easy job you left to your widower, being head of this household.

(Loud sound of toilet flushing and clanking noise in plumbing. He groans loudly and points upwards..)

Not to mention taking care of my older sister who lives upstairs and who's fifty-one cards short of a full deck.

JOEY. Auntie Rose is up from her nap. And when is the plumber coming to fix the pipes?

(Benny points to a date on the calender which is on the refrigerator door)

BENNY. Not soon enough! She uses enough water in two weeks to float the Q.E. Two, and if they had 'em, the Three and Four!!

JOEY. She can't help it. Father Martino says she's unique; what is known as a true eccentric.

BENNY. Don't get me started. I've been coping with that "true eccentric" all my life.

JOEY. Father Martino says she is living proof that God has a sense of humor and we should appreciate it and relish it.

BENNY. Yeah, well, you tell Father Martino I'm gonna die laughin', and the only relish I appreciate is on my hot dog. Set a place for her, too.

JOEY. You don't have to tell me. I set a place for her every night, don't I?

BENNY. She likes three forks. Give 'em to her.

JOEY. You're doing it again! I *always* give her three. Stop telling me!

BENNY. Wait. I changed my mind. We'll eat in the dining room.

JOEY. PHOOEY!! That's even more work. And I get stuck with it! I'm tired of being treated like week-old… left-over meatloaf!

(The phone rings. Joey hurries to the phone with great anticipation)

Hello?

(Very disappointed)

Oh. Sorry. Wrong number.

(Hangs up)

Darn it!

BENNY. For cryin' out loud! It was only a wrong number. Why the long puss?

JOEY. Leave me alone.

(Off. Door opening and slamming. Happy chatter in the outer hall of girls just arriving from work)

DODIE. *(Sing-song)* Hel-lo in there. We're ho-me.

BENNY. They're here. Set the table.

JOEY. I hate setting the table. That's a woman's work.

BENNY. Whatever happened to that nice, twelve year-old kid who used to live here?!

JOEY. See! That's how much attention you pay to me. I might as well be the wall paper. All I hear is… "Joey, take out the garbage…. Joey, set the table…. Joey, get the grated cheese." If I didn't do those things, you wouldn't notice me at all.

BENNY. What are you talking about?

JOEY. You don't even know how old I am.

BENNY. Didn't I just ask about the twelve year old kid who used to live here?!

JOEY. He still lives here, Pop… only now he's *thirteen*.

BENNY. *(To the ceiling)* That's explains it, Lenora. He's is *pub*-erty.

JOEY. *(Raises an arm and points to his arm pit)* For your information, it's pronounced "pew-berty. And I'm growing hair… and not just under my arms, either

BENNY. For Pete's sake, **quiet!** Your sisters are gonna hear. You're gettin' to be as looney as your aunt.

(Regina enters, dressed stylishly to show off her good figure and legs. Both she and Dodie are extremely attractive young women and have copious, elaborate hair-do's.)

REGINA. *(Kisses Benny on the cheek)* Good afternoon, Joey. Good afternoon, Dad.

BENNY. Good afternoon. You know, Regina, if you'd look down the rack two inches more, you might find a dress that fits. That one's a little snug, ain't it?

REGINA. *(To Joey)* I guess I know what kind of a mood he's in.

JOEY. Boy, am I glad you're home. Now Pop has someone else to pick on.

(Dodie enters. She is dressed in a very tight-fitting pants outfit)

DODIE. M-m-m. Something smells delicious in here. Must be Italian.

REGINA. Do we ever have anything else?

BENNY. When you have Italian, you don't need anything else. Still with the tight pants, Dodie? It's wonder your eyeballs don't bulge outta their sockets.

DODIE. *(Ignores him)* O-o-o-h. Black olives! I *love* black olives.

(She sticks two on her finger tips and waggles them at him. He looks up at the ceiling)

BENNY. See, Lenora? They listen with deaf ears, your children.

DODIE. *(She sits on a bar stool)* Hi-ya, Joey. Oh, no! You're not still doing homework!

JOEY. You could call it that.

REGINA. *(Removes her high heels)* I always did mine. Got it in on time and got excellent grades, too. That's undoubtedly why I'm one of the youngest supervisors at the phone company today.

(Exits, carrying her high heels)

DODIE. Oh, I hated it and never did mine. I mean, what was the point? I never gave them the answers they wanted anyway.

JOEY. I will never figure out to my dying day how you managed to graduate.

DODIE. Because that Mr. Delaney was a real doll. I will always be *indented* to him. He said, "Dolores Scrivente, the world needs to know that people with the level of your intelligence really exist." So he passed me. *(Eats another olive.)*

But when I got to beauty school, I found out what *real* homework was. Did you know you have to learn all the parts of the body, especially the head, the muscles and the *tendrils*?

JOEY. *(Constantly annoyed at DODIE's simple-mindedness)* TENDONS!

DODIE. Exactly. And... *(wiggling her fingers in the air)*... whattaya call those hootchie-jiggers that palpate everywhere?

JOEY. *(Shouts at her in disgust)* Could you possibly mean NERVES!

DODIE. *(Thinking)* Wait. Or is it cart'ledge?

JOEY. Cartilage doesn't *palpate!*

(He exits)

DODIE. *(Follows Joey and shouts after him)* Oh, no?! Well, Mr. Smartest-One-In-The Whole-Class.... ***mine*** does!

(Crosses to Benny)

Hi, Daddy. How's your hernia feeling?

BENNY. Lumpy and sore.

DODIE. Aw, poor Daddy. Where's Aunt Rose? She coming down to help with dinner?

BENNY. *(Looks upward)* Are you kidding? When's the last time *she* cooked anything.

(Regina enters wearing pink slippers and waves a greeting card at Benny)

REGINA. Oh, before I forget, Daddy, sign this card for cousin Theresa's baby shower.

BENNY. Forget it. She ain't even married and they're givin' her a shower?

REGINA. *(She insists)* Daddy, please!

(Benny signs the card)

Stop talking and just tell us what's for dinner?

BENNY. A new recipe that I'm developin' for the restaurant. And, special for you, I created Cacciatora Leanora; low cholest-roil, marinated in Marsala wine and smothered under a Putanesca sauce.

REGINA. *(Chiding him)* But Daddy, in Italian, doesn't Putanesca mean "little whore."

(She and Dodie giggle. Joey enters)

BENNY. *(Rhapsodically)* In my restaurant it'll mean fresh linguine swimming in a spicy marinara sauce fit for a king.

DODIE. *What* restaurant?

BENNY. Mine. Some day, as soon as I finish saving for both your weddings, I'm gonna have my own little trat-a-ria. I'm not gonna work for the post office forever, you know. Even widowers got dreams.

DODIE. *(Crosses and sits at table)* Oh, Daddy, by the time you save enough for a restaurant, you'll be too old to remember what it was you were saving for. So that's why my sweetie, Mario, and his family want to invest in one with you. I told them all about you and your dream. It really spooked their interest.

JOEY. *Spooked?* Try *sparked*, why don't you?

DODIE. *(Screeches at him)* Oh, what's the difference!!

JOEY. Pop, she *must* have sucked on lead paint chips!!

BENNY. *(Sits at table with Dodie)* Quiet, Mr. Wise Guy! We're talkin' here. So Dodie...you say that Mario is interested in a restaurant with me?

DODIE. Mostly his family. But the extremity has to look just right.

BENNY. Joey, translate please.

JOEY. She means *exterior*.

DODIE. That's what I said. They want one with a good front.

BENNY. I'd like a nice lookin' place, too.

REGINA. *(Sits at the table and begins painting her nails)* Sorry, Dad. I won't be here for dinner. I'm going out.

BENNY. I worked all afternoon on this dinner. And why can't you do your nails at Dodie's shop? She's got a whole beauty *saloon* at her finger tips and you have to do them at the table?

DODIE. Honestly, Daddy! If you were a woman, I'd swear you had T.S.P!

BENNY. Would my life be more meaningful if I knew what the hell she was talkin' about?

REGINA & JOEY. No!

DODIE. She'd have to make an appointment like everybody else. I'm very busy at the shop... with all the cuts, colors, shampoos, manicures and facials. Not to mention the waxings. I swear, I've yanked out enough hair this year to carpet Mt. Ernest up one side and down the other.

JOEY. *(Shouting at her)* Mount Everest.

DODIE. *Including* it. I tell you, it's exhausting. I never have time for myself.

BENNY. You. Get started in the dining room.

JOEY. See what I mean! Joey… do this… Joey… do that! There's more to me than just someone who takes up space in this house who knows how to set the dining room table.

DODIE. Why are we eating in the dining room? Is it a holy day, or something?

(Excitedly)

I *love* Holy Days!

JOEY. No one loves Holy Days. Unless you're a freaking nun!

(Joey exits. Benny calls after him.)

BENNY. Keep it up! That mouth is gonna bite you in the backside some day.

REGINA. What's going on, Daddy?

BENNY. Nothing! Why can't we just have a nice dinner in the dining room on a regular week night?

REGINA. I had a late lunch. Erwin treated me. Erwin Feingold.

BENNY. Erwin? Whatever happened to Makmoud?

REGINA. Oh. It's too depressing. They mistook him for an undesirable alien and they deported him, but that's old news. Anyhow, Erwin took me to this charming, little French place. I had Caesar salad and he had Oysters Napoleon.

BENNY. *(Hopefully)* Oh, yeah? This Erwin guy. Is there anything serious happening there?

REGINA. Relax, Dad. We're just co-workers. I got him

promoted to Area Code Manager of the Burroughs of Brooklyn and the Bronx.

BENNY. Let me guess. This one's Jewish. Right?

REGINA. You have a problem with that?

(Joey enters and stands listening)

BENNY. No, I don't have a problem with that. But last time it was a Pakistani. Before that a Romanian gypsy, and before that...

REGINA. He wasn't a gypsy.

BENNY. You could have fooled me, with that *hula-hoop* for an earring.

REGINA. So he was eclectic in his dress.

BENNY. If that means *weird*, you got my vote. And…. before *that* an Eye-ranian. And what about that guy from…. what the heck was the name of that place? Bandaid Sarah's Booger Tongue?

JOEY. Bandar Seri Begawan.* The capital of Brunei. Two-thousand, two-hundred and twenty six square miles; population 374,577.

(Joey picks up salt & pepper shakers and exits)

REGINA. Will you look at that. He definitely inherited my propensity for retention of facts .

DODIE. Wow. The only thing I retain is water.

(Sound of toilet flushing and clanking noise in plumbing)

BENNY. *(Rushes to doorway and shouts)* The pipes, Rose. The pipes! Have mercy, will ya?

DODIE. Regina, tell Daddy how you meet all these guys.

REGINA. It's no secret. On the telephone.

BENNY. WHAT?

REGINA. Daddy, it's all perfectly innocent. A gentlemen calls because he requires the service of a telephone company supervisor. I go, "Hel-lo-o. How may I assist you?" He tells me. I assist. We banter back and forth a

---

* *(BAN-dar Serrie BEG-a-wahn)*

little and before you know it, he's axing if he can meet me after work somewhere.

BENNY. Just like that!

REGINA. It's intriguing to visualize the face that accompanies the voice at the other end of the line… to hear the **timb-er** of a male voice expressing interest in axing to meet you. And the moment of confrontation is monumentally stimulating.

(She shrugs)

It's a hobby.

BENNY. You call that a hobby? My God, you're taking your life in your hands. You could be meeting up with an axe murderer!

(To the ceiling)

Hear that, Lenora? Hear what your first-born daughter is doing for kicks?

REGINA. What is your problem?

(Joey enters and picks up the napkin holder. He listens)

BENNY. For crying out loud. Just make a decision, will you? You're twenty-four years-old. With this *smorgasbord* of male admirerers, how hard can it be to pick one out and fall in love?

REGINA. You're making me sound ancient! I'm just launching my journey of discovery.

BENNY. *(Shakes his finger at her)* Well, discover this! By the time your mother was twenty-four, she already had you. And not only that…

JOEY. …she was *gravid* with Dodie.

BENNY. Quiet. This is just between us girls.

REGINA. Look, Daddy, what's wrong with wanting to encounter every type of person and culture before I decide who's right? So far, something is always lacking. I require someone brainy, an intellectual with depth who can appreciate my aptitude. Someone I can look up to, but he must be more cerebral than I.

BENNY. That's all peachy-keen, sweetheart, but you failed to mention the most important thing!

REGINA. And what would that be?

BENNY. *Love!* I mean, I *axe* you! Isn't that supposed to figure in somewhere?

REGINA. It would be *wonderful,* but I have yet to meet anyone with whom I could fall deeply in love.

BENNY. How can you tell, the way you flit from one guy to another.

REGINA. I'd rather stay single than just *settle* like so many other people. Experts say when it's right, you get this distinctive feeling inside. So far, I haven't felt anything special because no one that meaningful has materialized.

DODIE. Oh, Regina, make it simple. Daddy, what she's trying to illoom-istrate is that she has yet to find the guy who plops the cherry on her hot fudge sundae.

JOEY. Dodie ought to know. She's the queen of *illoomistration.*

DODIE. *(Rises, crosses to sink. Opens door underneath and discards her chewing gum)*

It comes natural. Mr. Delaney always said, "Dolores Scrivente, if you have any talent at all, it's for inducing things to their lowest, common denomination.

(Crossing to counter, she leans over it)

You know... I'm not meaning to brag... but me and Mario fell in love instantly. He was in the bowl and I was shampooing him. He said when I leaned over his face, he didn't even feel the protein conditioner I spilled in his eyes.

REGINA. Maybe I'll never find the man in my mind.

DODIE. His *coronas* burned for two days.

REGINA. Maybe I'll never get married.

DODIE. He had to get drops from the proctologist.

(Joey collapses in a chair with frustration.)

JOEY. The rest of my life can't come fast enough!

REGINA. Maybe I'll have to spend the rest of *my* life just "experiencing.

BENNY. Listen, I want to get on with my life, too. We all need love. It's like the garlic in the dip, or in the sauce, the thickening in the gravy. You can get by without it, but why would you want to? With those little things added, you're talking… *major satisfaction.*

(A beat)

Not only that, why do you think people write all them sad songs about how love ex-capes them? Then if they find it and then *lose* it, broken-hearted, they throw themselves off a bridge or jump in front of a train.

DODIE. Or a large truck.

JOEY. You must stay awake at night thinking up things that don't make sense.

(He exits to the dining room)

DODIE. *(She shouts after him)* I do not! My brain is always asleep even before I hit the pillow!

REGINA. Daddy, you just don't understand me. I enjoy a variety of exotic men and I will continue my odyssey.

BENNY. Regina, this may be a completely revolutionary idea to you, but have you ever considered a good old, fashioned, pure-blooded, Italian-American! There are three or four left in the Bronx, you know. Even your sister managed to find one.

(Exits into the dining room)

REGINA. *(Follows to door and calls after him)* Hah! You're holding Mario up as an example? I don't mean to cast aspersions, but she also found one who's had two wives. Not to mention those three bratty kids.

DODIE. Regina! You're being mean! I *love* those kids like they was my own.

REGINA. Good. Because you're going to be cutting their hair for the rest of your life. Not only do they not pay, they don't even *tip!* And, you're in line to be wife number four. How long do you think *that* will last?

DODIE. Regina Scrivente! You're going to be my maid-of-honor and you're my only sister. You're supposed to stand up for me.

REGINA. I do, honey. I adore you, but you're my little sister and I worry about you. You're so naive, so obtuse.

DODIE. Hey!! My weight is right where it should be!

REGINA. Oh, Dodie, just try to *concentrate* for a minute, will you?

DODIE. You know I get a headache if I concentrate too much.

REGINA. I'm the last person in the world who would want to inflict pain on you, but what I am trying to tell you is that you believe everything that everyone tells you.

DODIE. Not everything.

REGINA. And you *love* everything! No matter who or what, good or bad… you *love* it. That's not normal.

DODIE. I can't help it. That's the way I am.

REGINA. I just hate to see you get saddled with a lothario.

DODIE. Oh! You're lucky because I would probably get mad at you if I knew what that meant.

REGINA. Mario's got it made. He takes advantage of you.

DODIE. He does not.

REGINA. How many times does he ask you to baby-sit when he can't find a sitter?

DODIE. I like to sit. They read story books to me.

(Benny and Joey enter from dining room)

REGINA. I still say he's using you.

DODIE. He's going to set me up in my own shop, isn't he? We're already looking for an establishment. We even picked out the name.

(Gestures to the imaginary sign)

"Dodie's Do's – Unisex for Everyone."

(Joey clutches his throat and makes gagging and coughing sounds)

DODIE. Dadd-ee! Make him stop. He's disgusting.

BENNY. The table, Mr. Goof-Off!

JOEY. I'll bet Eugene O'Neill's father never chased him out of the kitchen. Or Arthur Miller's or William Saroyan's either!

BENNY. What have your friends got to do with this? They show up..I'll throw them *all* out..

JOEY. It's not fair. I am being wasted in a desert devoid of intellect!

BENNY. Wanna see *waste?* Just keep standing there, Joey. I'll show you waste.

(Benny takes a threatening step toward him)

JOEY. I am not defeated. This is only strengthening my determination.

(He exits.)

BENNY. *(To the ceiling)* If that means pig-headed, Lenora, he gets it from your side of the family.

(Throws his hands up in frustration.)

What the heck were we talking about?

REGINA. Mario. I say... so far, Mario is all *talk*.

DODIE. He is not! He gave me this solitaire, didn't he? We're getting married in October, aren't we? And he promised that someday he would buy me a house with a white *pivot* fence.

BENNY. At least *she's* getting married. Get off her case.

REGINA. I hope I'm wrong, but I think she's making a big mistake.

DODIE. My Mario has a lot of wonderful *quantities*.

REGINA. Oh, sure. Let's face it. There's a lot that would attract a female.

(She rattles them off)

He's handsome, charismatic, sexy, smooth, dresses

sharp and has a big car, and all that, but just answer me one thing.

DODIE. What?

(Joey enters. Picks up some silverware but stops to listen)

REGINA. What makes you so absolutely positive he loves you?

DODIE. Because I, and I alone... am responsible for plopping the cherry on **his** hot fudge sundae.

BENNY. Will you watch it? Your kid brother's in the room.

JOEY. I already know about plopping the cherry.

BENNY. WHAT?

JOEY. I heard Mario tell her.

(They all look at him in shocked silence)

I was hiding behind the couch. Okay??

DODIE. Oh, you deserve a good licking!

JOEY. I can't help it. I still have a child's natural curiosity.

BENNY. You gotta be kiddin'! Do you do that a lot? Hide behind the couch?

JOEY. Ye-ah, Pop. A *lot*. My teacher says I have been blessed with an inquiring mind.

BENNY. *(Furious)* Boy-oh-boy! Before this night is over, someone around here is gonna be blessed with a good swift kick.

JOEY. It's for *research and analysis,* all right?

BENNY. How about researching and analyzing the dining room table! Now get out there.

JOEY. I'm nothing but a slave around here. Someday I'm going to write a documentary about my dysfunctional childhood and I hope you can live with the guilt when you're old and wrinkled. *(Joey exits as Benny calls after him)*

BENNY. You're lucky you've got a childhood at all! That year, it was either you or a new Chevy!

(Same sounds of toilet flushing. Benny rushes to hallway door)

Rose! For crying out loud. The water bill. And save some water so we can do the dishes, will you?

REGINA. There's something else that bothers me about Mario. When is he going to get a job?

DODIE. He has one. He's a ***temporary fork-lifter.***

REGINA. That's what bothers me. How can he afford that big car or those clothes being a temp on a loading dock? There's nothing wrong with it, but when is he going to get a *real* job?

DODIE. He doesn't have to. He says he's connected.

BENNY. Connected?

DODIE. Well... almost, anyway. And when he's completely connected, he won't have to fork-lift anymore.

BENNY. Connected to what?

DODIE. To a family.

BENNY. Course he is. To his own... like we are.

DODIE. Oh, no. This is a special one.

REGINA. *How* special?

BENNY. *(Becoming suspicious)* All right, sweetheart, do you remember the name of this special family?

DODIE. I keep forgetting. But I get a mental picture.

REGINA. You don't have to concentrate, Dodie. Just gather all of your thoughts real hard and think.

DODIE. *(Squints, concentrates and squeals with laughter when she realizes she can do it)*

Oh, I can *do* that! I can *do* that!

REGINA. Okay. Can you describe the mental picture?

DODIE. Yeah. It reminds me of that movie.

REGINA. What movie?

DODIE. You know. The one with the little fawn.

REGINA. Oh! Oh! I know.

(She snaps her fingers)

The... "The Yearling."

(Dodie smiles as if in assent, and then frowns)

DODIE. No. No. The cartoon one, where the little fawn's mother gets shot by the hunters and everyone in the audience cries for an hour.

REGINA. Bambi?

DODIE. That's the one.

BENNY. The Bambi family... whoever heard of the Bambi family?

(Joey, who has been eavesdropping, rushes in and shouts.)

JOEY. Geez, Pop!! You don't have to be a rocket scientist to know she means ***The Bambino Family.***

DODIE. Yeah. That's them. Ever heard of them?

BENNY. *(Shocked)* THE BAMBINO FAMILY??? THE SARLO BAMBINO FAMILY?

DODIE. Oh, you know them. Are they paesans*, or something?

BENNY. Not any of ours!

JOEY. You'd have to be dead and buried not to know them.

BENNY. A lot of people got that way because they did know them! Now, Dodie, what makes you say Mario is a member of the... *(He looks around and whispers loudly)*... the Bambino Family?

DODIE. *(She whispers back)* I heard him talking.

BENNY. Where?

DODIE. *(Whispers again)* On the phone.

BENNY. *(Shouts)* For crying out loud. I can't hear you! Speak up.

DODIE. Don't yell at me. I didn't do anything. What did I do?

BENNY. All right. I'm sorry, I'm sorry. You didn't do anything. Just tell us.

DODIE. I heard him on the phone, in a booth in the drugstore. The one next door to his apartment. I went in to get my birth control pills.

* pronounced pi-ZAHNS

BENNY. Oh, geez! Don't tell me that.

DODIE. Oh, it's all right, Daddy. I just buy them. I never *use* them.

BENNY. Oh, God! This is gonna kill me.

REGINA. Ignore him, Dodie. Then what happened?

DODIE. Well, when I walked back to meet him, I overheard him talking. That's all.

(She throws up her hands)

Everything is on the up-and-up. Why are you acting this way?

BENNY. If everything is on the up-and-up, how come he made the call from a booth instead of his apartment or from his cell phone?

DODIE. I don't know. I think there was an exterminator up there. Yeah. That's what it was. I remember now. He said something about "bugs" in his apartment.

BENNY. Dodie, is this the same family that wants to invest in a restaurant?

DODIE. Uh, huh! Wouldn't that be so fun?

BENNY, REGINA & JOEY. *OH, MY GOD!*

DODIE. I don't know why everyone is so excited. They're very nice people. I even met some of them.

BENNY. You met them? *The Bambinos?* I don't believe it. Where?

DODIE. At a little restaurant in Manhattan. They were very gentlemanly and handsomely *expired in black, sharkskin suits*. They made me feel extra special. They like... really *scrupulized* me... and asked all kinds of questions.

REGINA. What kind of questions?

DODIE. Oh, like... how long did I know Mario, was I going to marry him, and would I *stay* married to him, and did I like lots of children. Oh, and did I have to know where my husband was every single minute. I said *no* because, after all, absence makes the heart a *fondler*.

(A beat)

And then they wanted to know all about my family. Especially *you*, Daddy.

BENNY. Me? Oh, no. What did you tell them?

DODIE. Oh, how good you take care of us, especially since Mamma died, and how hard you work at the post office to save money for your tra-tor-eo. And how *flus-trating* it is because your boss, Mr. Mulroney, is a tot-al moron.... with no gool-yonies whatsoever.

BENNY. Oh, geez! Why did you say that?

DODIE. That's what you tell us all the time.

BENNY. Do you even know what goolyonies *are*?

DODIE. Mario says they're Italian prairie oysters. I've never seen any, but then I've never seen a prairie, either.

REGINA. Oh, Dodie! What did they say after that?

DODIE. They said.... after they laughed a lot..... .

(Trying to remember)

...they said... oh, tell Daddy not to worry; that someone might be in touch with Daddy soon about a restaurant. One with a very low overhead.

(Makes a big, sweeping gesture overhead)

Although I always liked those *cauldron* ceilings myself... don't you?... and then, I also told them about your hernia.

BENNIE. She... told... them... about my hernia, Lenora.

REGINA. I'm sure they found *that* fascinating.

DODIE. Oh, they did. Especially when I told them it was located... *(points directly)*... in your *groan*.

(Benny moans loudly.)

JOEY. I just realized why some kids my age run away from home.

DODIE. And they said to tell Daddy if his doctor couldn't fix him, they know one who could, and then they know someone who could fix his doctor.

BENNY. Oh, God! Who did you talk to? What were their names?

DODIE. Angelo… and a Tony, or something. I don't remember. One was a captain, or lieutenant, I think. Yeah. That's what he was. They all had names that sounded like they belong on a box of macaroni. But the most important man there was even *higher* up.

BENNY. How high?

DODIE. He's so high, they call him only by his nick-name. I mean, *I* never heard of him before, but I never heard of William Shakespeare, either. I thought he was dead until I heard they revived him in Central Park.

(A beat)

He probably keeled over jogging.

BENNY. HOW THE HECK DID SHAKESPEARE GET INTO THIS?

DODIE. Don't yell. You're upsetting me.

BENNY. Okay… okay. Just tell us about the "high" guy, will ya!

DODIE. All right. I *loved* him!

REGINA. She's off and running!

JOEY. Tell us his nick-name.

DODIE. Listen to this. It is *so* cute.

(A beat)

"The Don." Isn't that cute? Just… "The Don."

BENNY. That's it. We're dead.

DODIE. That family must really cherish him. They were very protective of him, and just sort of surrounded him all of the time. And you know what? When he stood up, they *all* stood up. And when he sat down, they *all* sat down. And he said "Che* bedda" a lot. What does that mean, Daddy?

BENNY. It means "Run. Don't walk..to the nearest cemetery."

REGINA. What else about The Don?

---

* *pronounced KAY*

DODIE. Oh. This was so sweet. He even made up a little pet name for me. "Merry... Lynn." Isn't that cute? "Che bedda, Merry Lynn." I was tot'lly flattered. He was so adorable. His nose came just up to... here... on me. *(Indicates her bosom)* You should have seen his eyes twinkle then.

REGINA. I'll just bet! The dirty old geezer!

DODIE. And then he said... well, I don't know what he said because they all started to talk Italian. And Mario said a bunch of stuff back in Italian too, which was a surprise because I had no idea he was that *fluid*. But this is the thrilling and heart-warming part... they all took turns kissing him on both cheeks.

BENNY. Don't look now but we're up to our collective "goolyonies" in trouble.

DODIE. *(Totally distressed)* Oh... Mario made me swear that I would never tell anyone, but I just did. What'll I do? What'll I do?

REGINA. Dodie, listen to me. Look right into my eyes. What do you see?

DODIE. *(Looks closely)* I **love** that new eye shadow.

REGINA. *(Out of patience and shouts)* For goodness sake, Dodie! Will you concentrate!! What you see is a sister who loves you and is trying to help.

DODIE. All right! But I'm starting to get that headache.

REGINA. You're going to have to tell him. It's best that he knows that we know. That way, you wouldn't have to lie. Besides, you never did know how to lie.

DODIE. Well, it was an accident, wasn't it? It just slipped out. It doesn't count if it just slips out. I remember that from Sister Mary Frances in Cataclysm.

BENNY. Oh, God! I'm in a corner. That's what. What do I do now, Lenora?

(Becomes assertive)

Wait a minute. Why am I asking? I'm the father here, right? I'm the head of this household. I make the decisions. I know what I have to do. Call the caterers! I'm stopping the wedding.

DODIE. Dad-d-e-e... why would you do a terrible thing like that?

JOEY. P-s-s-t. Pop. Better leave it alone. If you mess things up, he could have you fit for a pair of cement shoes.

BENNY. Oh, no! I never thought about that.

(He picks up a bottle of Mylanta and takes a couple of swigs out of the bottle)

Thank you, God. On top of everything else, now I got a good case of acido.*

DODIE. Oh, Daddy, see how we aggravate you? If you'd only let Regina and I move out on our own, you'd be much happier and could live peacefully with only Joey to drive you crazy.

BENNY. Forget it. Especially not after what you just told us.

DODIE. We would come every Sunday for dinner. You could practice on us for the restaurant.

BENNY. What restaurant?! It was all just a pipe dream. I'll be lucky if I live long enough to end up on a park bench feeding the squirrels leftover meatballs.

(To the ceiling)

No way outta this mess, Lenora.

(He drops to his knees)

One way or another, I'm doomed. Blood-pressure or bullets.

(He squeaks tearfully)

They're gonna kill me.

JOEY. Uh-uh. Wrong.

BENNY. Hah?

JOEY. They don't always use bullets, Pop.

BENNY. Who?

JOEY. The mob. One of their favorite methods is the garrotte.

* *pronounced AH-je-da*

BENNY. The what?

(Joey moves toward Benny and stands behind him)

JOEY. Garrotte. It originated as a collar of torture in the Spanish Inquisition.

BENNY. *(Still on his knees)* How does it work?

(Joey places his hands around Benny's neck)

JOEY. It causes death by strangulation with a rope or wire. It's quieter and cheaper. And more difficult to trace. No bullets, no guns… no serial numbers.

(With relish, Joey mimes being strangled, gasping and sticking his tongue out)

BENNY. *(Bends over in pain)* O-oh!

REGINA. Now look what you've done, Joey. You've exacerbated his groin. Come and sit, Daddy.

(Regina and Dodie get him up and lead him to a chair. They fuss over him)

Are you wearing that truss Auntie Rose bought you?

BENNY. No! It's too uncomfortable! Look, I'm all right. I just yelled too hard.

JOEY. That's right. With any luck, you could die from a strangulated hernia.

REGINA & DODIE. JOEY!

BENNY. OH-OHH!

(Enter Aunt Rose. She and Benny make an impromptu duet with their "oh's)

AUNT ROSE. O-H-H!

(Rose is dressed in a brightly colored caftan, with a colorful decoration in her hair. She slumps against the door frame dramatically, echoing the same "oh" sound as Benny. She is holding out a red water bottle/enema bag and heads for the sink.)

I had a *dream!* It was something all right!

JOEY. About what, Aunt Rose?

BENNY. Oh, he had to ask! And how many times have I told you not to fill that thing in the kitchen sink. Do it in the bathroom.

ROSE. The sink is too small. It squirts me in the eye balls.

DODIE. Then how about the bathtub?

ROSE. It hurt my back when I bend over.

BENNY. *(Shouts at her)* You don't enter my kitchen until you get rid of that thing!

ROSE. All right... all right.

(She tosses the enema bag under the sink and slams shut the cabinet door)

Happy now?

(She turns, stops and looks around. Palms upward, she senses something.)

Hey, wait a minute! What's going on in here? The atmosphere in this room is heavy and pulsating. Benny, you been eating sauerkraut, again?

BENNY. No, I haven't been eating sauerkraut!

JOEY. Come on, Auntie Rose. Tell us about the dream, will you?

ROSE. *(Kisses Joey on the cheek)* Oh, how I love this boy. He and I are on the same plane. You've got the gift, Joey. You're an old soul, kid. You've been around the "karmic" block before. And marked for greatness, may I add.

BENNY. Will you stop filling his head with that garbage? He's gettin' to be as bad as you.

ROSE. Joey understands who I am... why I must keep my body, this vessel, my instrument.... purged; spotless from impurities so I may receive messages from La-lu-pa-ta-la'-la. And who is La-lu-pa-ta-la'-la? He is my entity. A Tibetan monk who died in...

ALL. ...the... Second Century... A. D.

DODIE. *(With genuine sincerity)* How *is La-lu*-poo-poo or whatever... Aunt Rose? Heard from him lately?

ROSE. Thank you for asking, sweetheart. If you never ask, you never learn. Not one day goes by that I don't pick up his vibrations.

(She sticks her finger in her ear and wiggles it)

He makes a buzzing sound in my ear, and I know it won't be long before I get, what I call, an Ear-mail. For I, and I alone, have been chosen to be his channel.

DODIE. You mean... like on cable?

ROSE. You got it. Only it's from a Divine Network.

BENNY. *Nutwork* is more like it.

ROSE. Scoff if you must. Ridicule. I'm used to it. Did you ever wonder why I got fired from so many jobs?

BENNY. No one cares, Rose. We got bigger problems.

ROSE. Because I always knew who was stealing the scotch tape and the Number Two pencils, and which boss was schtupping what secretary. Oh, it's a gift. Joey has this gift, too, if only he chooses to develop it.

JOEY. *(Impatiently)* Just tell us the dream, Auntie Rose.

ROSE. Oh, it was something all right. Are you ready? First, there were palm trees, bending and swaying in the breeze.

(She sways dramatically)

And then came the limos. L-o-n-g ones. Then I heard music. Glissandos, and crescendos, trills and obbligatos; whole symphonies. And there were lights. Cascades of them. I was floating.... floating. I thought I had died and gone to heaven. And last, came the applause. Lots of it. People were shouting... something... but I can't remember what it was.

JOEY. *(Greatly disappointed)* Aw, geez, Auntie Rose!

ROSE. Oh, it'll come, Joey. It always does. I was born with a cowl, you know. I'm psychic. I can tell things.

BENNY. Well, tell yourself it's time for dinner and sit down. I'm not eating. I suddenly lost my appetite.

ROSE. What are you? Crazy? I can't eat now. Besides, I have to get myself ready so I can go to Bingo. Mary LaMotta is going to win the hundred dollar jackpot and she owes me ten bucks.

REGINA. Erwin and I are going to catch the new Roger DePiro movie.

JOEY. *(Excited)* You are! *Roger DePiro?!* He's my idol. Can I come, too? I promise I won't spy. I'll just sit and stare at the screen.

REGINA. Sorry, Joey. Some other time.

JOEY. Sorry, Joey... sorry Joey! Big sisters are supposed to indulge their kid brothers. Well, it's beneath me to beg, but some day... you'll be begging *me* for favors!

REGINA. Are you coming down with something? Go take an aspirin!

(Rose suddenly raises one finger. There is silence, as she squints her eyes.)

ROSE. *Wait!* Don't anyone move. I'll get the phone.

(A beat. The phone rings. Rose rushes to phone and picks it up. She listens briefly.)

You've got the wrong number.

(She slams the receiver down)

JOEY. Are you sure it wasn't for me?

ROSE. No! It wasn't for you, but I had a flash. There's going to be a great upheaval in this house. Last week, someone kept calling and asking for a dead man, and I kept hanging up on him.

(Rose suddenly raises one finger. There is silence, as she squints her eyes.)

Wait! Someone get the door.

(A beat. The doorbell rings)

DODIE. Oh. Someone's at the door. I'll get it.

(She exits)

ROSE. Now, who can that be?

BENNY. You're the psychic. You tell *us*.

ROSE. Oh, oh.

JOEY. What's "oh - oh" mean?

(Voices can be heard at hallway door.)

ROSE. *(With great passion)* It's started.

REGINA. What's started?

ROSE. The upheaval! *Get ready.*

DODIE. *(Off)* But I tell you, there's no one here by that name.

VOICE. Are you sure? Are you absolutely sure? This is the address we were given.

BENNY. Dodie? What's going on out there.

(Dodie enters with Eviel Kharren following. He is dark, thirty-ish; extremely attractive and bookish-looking. Dressed in a business suit, wears horn-rimmed glasses; carries a brief case.)

DODIE. This gentleman is looking for someone at our house who isn't here.

EVIEL. Good-afternoon. The young lady is correct. I am looking for a person at this address. At least, it's the one I was given but we've been having difficulty making telephone contact. I apologize if I'm disturbing you at your dinner hour.

REGINA. *(Immediately attracted, she gives a throaty growl)* M-m-m-m. Not at all. Good afternoon to *you*.

BENNY. *(Alarmed)* Wait a minute. Are you a *cop?* Because if you are, we don't know anything. We are all completely ignorant.

EVIEL. Good heavens, no. Whatever gave you that idea?

(He glances down at piece of paper in his hand)

But I'm extremely baffled. This is the address, all right. Do you know of anyone in the neighborhood with this name?

DODIE. Not that I know of and we've lived here since time immoral.

REGINA. Permit me. How may I service you?

(She looks at it, leaning closely to him. She sniffs)

M-m-m-m. Your after-shave... "Trojan Knight." Gift from your wife?

EVIEL. Uh, no wife. Mother.

REGINA. Your mother. How liberated of her. I like that almost as much as your after shave.

ROSE. The only thing I smell is shish-ka-bob.

EVIEL. *(Impressed)* **Really?** You smell that?

REGINA. Aunt Rose, we're interrupting the gentleman.

(Leans over the paper)

Now, where were we? Oh, yes. That's our address all right, and our... uh... *my* phone number. Now, how may we assist you?

EVIEL. I'm looking for a... Mr. Dante.

(To Benny)

Are you Mr. Dante? And I do hope you are, sir, because if so, you have contributed something that could make a major impact on the world of theater. However, there seems to be something vital missing.

(Opens his brief case and pulls out a paper-filled binder and waves it in the air)

JOEY. What? What was missing?

BENNY. Will you stop butting in!

(To Eviel)

Who are you looking for?

ROSE. That voice. I'd recognize it anywhere. He's the one who's been asking for a dead man.

(She makes the sign-of-the-horns with her right hand and points it at him)

You're a little late, mister. In case you haven't noticed, your friend, Dante, has been dead since the thirteen-hundreds.

EVIEL. You're the lady who's been hanging up on me.

(Rose raises her "sign" higher. He steps closer.)

ROSE. Don't come any closer. That's far enough.

EVIEL. What... what is she doing?

DODIE. She's casting out your evil eye.

EVIEL. *(Alarmed)* I didn't know I had one.

BENNY. For crying out loud, Rose. Would you knock it off! You're scaring him.

REGINA. Aunt Rose, we're interrupting the proceedings here with mister... mister?

EVIEL. Oh. Kharren. Eviel Kharren. I'm a theatrical attorney.

(He reaches into his pocket and hold out his business card)

ROSE. *(Horrified)* Did you hear that? He said his name is "*EVIL*"

EVIEL. My name is pronounced that... that way but it's spelled like this. See?

(Holds a business card out to her)

There's an extra "e."

ROSE. Who in his right mind would name his kid "Evil?"

EVIEL. It's an old, but distinguished, Lebanese name. Really short for a much longer name.

REGINA. *Lebanese?* **FAS**-cinating. I've never known a person of the Lebanese persuasion.

(Looks pointedly at Benny)

EVIEL. Really? Well, if you investigated, you'd find us to be a romantic culture, bordering on the exotic.

REGINA. Oh... be still my heart!

EVIEL. And I'm afraid my last name is also short.... for a much, *much* longer name.

(A beat.)

Armenian.

AUNT ROSE. I *told* you I smelled shishkabab.

EVIEL. *Astonishing!* Do I detect a touch of the psychic in you?

AUNT ROSE. *(She raises one hand.)* Guilty, Your Honor. You see... I'm psychic and...

BENNY. No one gives a hot patootey, Rose Now... about this Mr. Dante guy.......

JOEY. *(Pokes Benny)* He's closer than he knows.

BENNY. *(Annoyed)* Will you *quit* with the pokin'.

JOEY. *(Joey pokes him again.)* He's so warm he's getting hot.

BENNY. I said cut it out!

EVIEL. Obviously I have incorrect information here. My apologies for disturbing you. I'll just pack up here and leave.

JOEY. NO! ***Wait.*** Don't go. I mean... maybe I could help you find him.

REGINA. Ignore him. He can't help, but I can... through the telephone company.

(She pushes him into a chair at the table and sits in the adjacent chair)

JOEY. Oh, no? My way is faster. Cheaper, too. He wouldn't have to buy me dinner or pay for the motel.

BENNY. *(Angrily)* Where is this stuff coming from?

JOEY. From a student of life... that's who.

EVIEL. I've already tried the phone company. The only information you get from the telephone company is that they can't give you any. Even talked to a supervisor.

REGINA. Did you talk to Supervisor Number Seven.... - *O- O-H-H?*

(Seductively breathy on "oh")

EVIEL. No... I mean, sh-sh-she didn't... she didn't say.

REGINA. Then, you didn't talk to *me*. I definitely would have remembered *your* tim-ber.

JOEY. I ask you. What does it take? Am I only the sane person in this house?

BENNY. Will you be quiet for five minutes! The world does not revolve around you.

ROSE. But it will... and soon!

(Rose suddenly raises one finger. There is silence, as she squints her eyes.)

Wait! *Quiet.* Someone get the door.

(A beat. The back doorbell rings)

DODIE. Oh, is this getting to be like Grand Central, or what? I'll get it.

(She begins to exit. At the door she stops. An intake of breath)

Maybe it's Mr. Dante. If it is, what'll I tell him.

BENNY. Tell him to go home! He's gonna have company.

JOEY. Don't worry. It's not him.

BENNY. Take a look at this! Now, the *kid* thinks he's psychic.

(Mario enters. He is muscularly macho, handsome, sharply dressed in a black leather jacket. He flexes.)

MARIO. Yo! The back door was unlocked. I don't like that. You never know what kind of trash could come walkin' in.

DODIE. Mario! Sweetheart. What a lovely surprise.

MARIO. Hi, doll!

DODIE. You're early.

(She runs to him and they kiss noisily on the lips with lots of m-m-m sounds. Benny slams a cabinet door hard to interrupt their smooching)

MARIO. Sorry, sugar, but I gotta be someplace later. Uh... one of them *club* things... you know?

BENNY. Whatever it is, we don't wanna hear, we don't wanna know.

MARIO. Hey, everybody.

(They respond)

Yo, Aunt Rose. How ya doin', babe? See anything interesting lately?

ROSE. Yeah. I see you've playing with the wise-guys again. One of these days, one of them is going to back you right into a corner.

MARIO. I love ya, too, Aunt Rose... but you got a wild imagination.

DODIE. Daddy... this is Mario.

BENNY. Geez, Dodie! In case you don't remember, we already met.

(He looks up at the ceiling)

Excuse me, Lenora, but do you see what I have to contend with around here?

EVIEL. *(Stops dead in his tracks)* What did you just say?

BENNY. Who?

EVIEL. You. You looked up there...

(Points at the ceiling)

and you said... something.

JOEY. He said "Excuse me for asking, Lenora, but do you see what I have to contend with around here?"

EVIEL. That's what I thought he said. Ladies and gentlemen, I have canceled my departure.

MARIO. What's that supposed to mean?

EVIEL. I am not leaving.

MARIO. Who is this guy? You want him to leave? I'll get rid of him for you.

(Pulls up him by the lapels)

EVIEL. How do you do. Eviel Kharren is my name and it's my obligation to tell you I have a black belt.

(He affects a silly-looking Karate move with a silly screech. Mario backs off.)

BENNY. *Please!* I expected a quiet dinner. *Not Murder Incorporated!*

ROSE. *(Holds up a finger)* **Wait!** Someone get the phone.

(A beat. The phone rings)

REGINA. Is she one for the books or what?

(Regina answers the phone and gets rid of Erwin very quickly.)

Hello? Oh... Erwin. What's the matter? Oh, that's too bad. Take care of yourself and feel better. Hear? Bye-bye.

(She hangs up)

What a shame. It seems that Erwin met his Waterloo. He's throwing up the Oysters Napoleon. That means I don't have a date tonight after all.

ROSE. *(With fingers to her head, and eyes closed, she beckons to Regina who crosses to her)*

Psst! I see you leaving here with someone in boxer shorts who has a shishkabab aura... and then your getting home in the wee hours after a meaningful evening of... uh... stimulation... intellectual and otherwise. Go for it, honey.

REGINA. A Lebanese in boxer shorts with brains *and* a vocabulary? Oh... God. What a turn-on. I don't have to be told twice. Well, Daddy, since Mr. Kharren insists upon remaining, and Mario has just arrived, I think it would be only polite to invite them to stay for dinner. Don't you?

BENNY. Hey! What's another couple of mouths? Joey, set two more places.

JOEY. Why me? Why do I have to set the places.

MARIO. *(Turns to Eviel)* Who is *this* guy? Who are you, anyway?

EVIEL. *(Removes a business card and hands it to him)*

I'm an attorney for Roger DePiro.

JOEY. *(Excited)* Wow! *Roger DePiro?*

MARIO. The actor?

EVIEL. Actor... producer... and director.

MARIO. So whatta ya' doin' here?

EVIEL. Looking for one Mr. Dante. And he's here. In this room.

MARIO. What's that... Dante? Some kinda code name?

EVIEL. I believe it's what's known in the business as a pseudonym. A nom de plume...

MARIO. A numb-de-whom?

JOEY. For crying out loud! Doesn't anyone around here recognize a pen name when they hear one?

MARIO. Oh! Like a phony moniker. An a.k.a.

EVIEL. Very astute. You must be in law enforcement.

MARIO. Who? *ME? A cop? Ha!* That's a good one.

BENNY. Yeah! HA is right! And we already told you, there ain't no Mr. Dante here...

JOEY. But Pop....

BENNY. Quiet. I'm talking.

EVIEL. To make it brief, I've been searching for the author of this.

(He opens his brief case and extracts the script and waves it)

ROSE. That's it! That's it! I remember now. That's what they were shouting. "Author... Author!" In the dream.... with the lights and the music. I knew it would come back. I was born with a cowl. I'm psychic you know.

BENNY. What the heck's psychic about that?

ROSE. Benny, in Italian, Scrivente means author.

BENNY. What's that got to do with us?

EVIEL. *(Holds up the script)* Probably this. A young messenger left *this* manuscript in the Manhattan office of Roger DePiro. Unsolicited. Mr. DePiro does not accept *unsolicited*. We can thank the receptionist who read it before it hit the waste basket.

(He opens the manuscript, stands)

If you will indulge me, may I read you some of the contents?

(They all agree. He clears his throat and begins to read, slowly and clearly.)

"It was Friday. She leaned him back on the couch, pressing her ample body over him, crushing his lips with hot kisses. He grappled with her because he knew someone would soon be entering the house and in his struggle to rise, he fell off the couch and a searing pain tore at his groin."

BENNY. *(Startled, he reacts with guilt)* Holy sweet jumpin' Saint Jude….

MARIO. Wow! This is good. Do more.

EVIEL. *(Pointedly)* "Lenora," he cried from a tortured soul as he looked up at the *ceiling*, "I've fallen in love with another woman. Can you ever forgive me?"

REGINA. Daddy? Is that *YOU?*

BENNY. I ain't Mr. Dante. I don't know nothin' about it.

(Looks up the ceiling)

Hear me, Lenora. It's all a pack of lies! I go to mass every Sunday and confession twice a year.

(He dips his finger in a pot of water on the stove and makes the Sign of the Cross)

I'm a good widower, I swear. Besides, if you met her, you'd like her, too!

EVIEL. There's a lot more packed in these pages, people. Although as yet untitled, this is the definitive saga, told in simple yet riveting narrative; the chronicle of a guileless, unspoiled, unsuspecting woman inextricably linked to the underworld through her muscled, philandering paramour; a ravishing business woman who uses her position and her sexual appetite to boost her male underlings up the corporate ladder…. the shame of the unwed cousin who suffers her pregnancy in silence until her married lover can free himself from a miserable marriage;… the clairvoyant matriarch of family who navigates the family's destiny through guidance from the occult. And, last but not least, the unappreciated, abused son, exploited by all in his struggle for love, acceptance, but most of all... recognition.

MARIO. Yo! This is really good. I especially like that muscled-guy part. Do more.

JOEY. *Really?* You really think it's *good?*

EVIEL. *Very.* To continue....

(Skips a few more pages. Dramatically...)

"**Gravid** with child, she leaned her bulging body against the glass counter...

(Joey recites a few words with him. Astonished, Eviel stops as Joey interrupts and recites alone.)

JOEY. *(Continuing and ending the speech)...* the glass counter filled with Kaiser Rolls and breathed in short, heavy pants, "Call an ambulance. My... time... has... come."

(There is silence as all stare at Joey in shock.)

EVIEL. A-h... ha!

(He puts one arm around Joey's shoulder, and points at him with his free hand and happily announces with a flourish.)

I believe we have found the illusive.... ***Mr. Dante.***

BENNY. *(To Eviel)* There's no Mr. Dante in this house!!

JOEY. Oh, Pop! There is, too. That's what I've been trying to tell everybody. I'm ***him.***

BENNY. Who?

JOEY. Pop! It's *me...* I'm *it...* I'm *him*!!!

BENNY. YOU? My son... has been writin' this porno material? How do you know about this stuff?

JOEY. You create recipes and I create stories from life!

REGINA. Oh! I would just like to know.... who is the character with the sexual appetite?!

JOEY. I said you were *ravishing!*

REGINA. Oh, yeah. I love her already.

BENNY. Why don't you write about dogs and horses... like normal kids!

JOEY. You wouldn't let me have a dog, let alone a horse! At school, the teacher says we should write about what we know, and I know a lot more than you think I know. Pop, in case you never heard, sex is normal! Even Father Martino says so.

BENNY. Someone had better restrain me.

ROSE. Harm one hair of Joey"s scalp and risk bringing a cosmic curse upon this family.

EVIEL. Why don't you calm down for a minute, Mr. Scrivente, and allow me. This is indeed unexpected. I'd like to talk to Joey, if you don't mind, and if it's all right with Joey.

JOEY. That'll be a switch! No one ever talks *to* me. They talk *at* me. Loud!

(He steers Joey to a seat. He shakes hands with him.)

EVIEL. How are you, Joey?

JOEY. Fine, thank you.

EVIEL. How old are you, son?

JOEY. Thirteen.

(Looks at his father accusingly!)

EVIEL. Tell me, Joey, is this the first thing you've written?

JOEY. Oh, no. I've been writing since I was a kid. Poems… short stories… stuff….

BENNY. I didn't know that. Why didn't you say something?

JOEY. No one ever asked. They always think I'm doing homework. But, my mother, Lenora… she's dead now, she said I had a gift and I should never stop writing because if you don't use your talent, God might get mad and take it away from you. I got enough people mad at me around here without getting God in on the act. 'Cause when God gets mad, all hell could break loose! *(He shrugs)*

But I never thought it was any good, what I wrote. But Mom said it was good, so I did it because it made her happy. And I liked to see her smile. I remember her smile.

(Chokes up)

I miss it... a lot... you know?

EVIEL. I know. Of course you do. And what made you write this?

JOEY. To make *me* happy. I wanted to show my family I can do something more than take out the trash, or set the table. They're always so busy with themselves, they never have time for me.

So, I started to put everything down on paper as it came. Of course, I do a lot of investigation.

(A beat)

I observe people while being concealed. You learn a lot that way. But, I only wanted to make them proud. Like my Mom was. You... know... something to make them sit up and notice.

EVIEL. Joey, do you realize the scope of what you have written?

JOEY. Not really. I only know I liked doing it. That's why I took it to Roger DePiro. He's my idol and I figured he would tell me the truth... if he knew he was my idol, and all. And I heard he likes kids. He must. He's got eight or nine with a bunch of different wives.

EVIEL. Joey, I'm going to ask you to trust me. And your family, too. Because I promise that we will take good care of you, and protect you. I will tell you what you've accomplished.

(He rises and speaks to the room.)

What we have here, ladies and gentlemen, is a perfect literary masterpiece; something so powerful, so intriguing, with multi-faceted dramatic potential, that Roger DePiro himself is offering to option this property with the intention of developing it into a blockbuster piece for the stage.... for ***Broadway.***

ROSE. *(Thrilled)* Didn't I tell you? Is that Joey an old soul or what!

EVIEL. He is gifted beyond belief and is to be revered as an

Italian-American prodigy along with other Italian treasures who have contributed to the world through all of the sciences and the arts. Puccini, Rossini, Michael Angelo, Leonardo DaVinci….

DODIE. *(With enthusiasm)* **Ray Romano!**

ROSE. This family can't see the palm trees for the jungle. Oh, yeah. Tell 'em where the palms trees come in.

EVIEL. After Broadway, comes the screen play… hence, Hollywood. However, there is no final chapter. We need to know how it ends. Ad when we do, comes the recognition and remuneration. To simplify it, we need Act Two, Joey.

JOEY. *That's* what was missing! Boy, I'll have to get busy, won't I?

DODIE. I'm so proud of you, my baby brother. From now on, you can hide behind the couch any time you want and even bring a friend.

(Both sisters kiss him… one on each cheek. Joey grimaces)

ROSE. See that? Let's be grateful and give thanks for Joey. Let's pray for Act Two. Let's eat!

BENNY. Wait a minute! Anyone reading that thing will think I was being disloyal to the memory of your wonderful mother.

REGINA. Oh, Daddy, relax. Even widowers are allowed a little extra-curricular activity.

ROSE. *(Holds up a finger)* Wait.

DODIE. What is it, Aunt Rose? The door or the phone?

ROSE. I don't know what this one is. It… feels different.

(Mario's cell phone [in his pocket] rings loudly to The God Father theme song)

MARIO. *(Also surprised)* Oh…. excuse me. My… my…. thing… here.

(Turns his back, moves away, pulls his cell phone from pocket and speaks quietly)

Yeah? What? WHAT?

(He listens; turns and looks at Dodie)

Yeah, she's here. What's up? Huh? You wanna talk to her? You wanna talk to *her*?

Are you sure? Oh... oh... no problem. No problem at all. Just a minute.

(Puzzled, motions to Dodie. She crosses to him and take the cell phone)

It's what's-his-name.... from the.... *club*... he wants to talk to you..... *Merry Lynn.*

DODIE. Me? O-h-h, I think I know why.

(Speaks into the phone)

Hello? Oh, hello, Lieutenant Angelo.

(To Mario)

It's Lieutenant Angelo.

MARIO. Sh-sh-sh-sh!

DODIE. H-m-m? Sure. No problem. Birthday cakes are easy. We'll do three candles.... one for the past, one for the present, and one for the future.

(She listens)

Oh. Just a minute. Let me check.

(She covers the mouthpiece. Unsure of herself)

Daddy.... is two o'clock Sunday good for you?

BENNY. What's two o'clock Sunday?

DODIE. Daddy... Mario.... I hope it's all right... and that you're not going to be mad at me. I forgot to tell you... I invited them all here for dinner on Sunday.

BENNY. *(Stuttering)* Who? The Bambin... the Bambin.... ?

MARIO. You did *what?*

REGINA. Dodie! You didn't!

JOEY. *(Thrilled)* ***ALL... RIGHT!!*** *Man, can I explore now!*

DODIE. Oh, *thanks,* Joey.

(Into the phone)

Two o'clock is fine. See you then. And have a light breakfast because my father is a wonderful cook. You'll be thrilled to be *assimilated* in the tra-tor-eo business with him. Oh, and say happy birthday to that cute little Don for me.

BENNY. Oh, my... God. I think I'm paralyzed. My legs won't work.

ROSE. *(Sticks a finger in each ear)* **Wait a minute**. Everyone be quiet. I'm getting an Ear-mail.

(Silence, as Rose closes her eyes and wiggles her fingers as he connects to La-la)

Uh.huh... uh... huh. Yeah. Yeah. I see. Gotcha.

(Removes her fingers.. Speaks to Eviel)

You. Whatta you doing at two o'clock on Sunday?

EVIEL. Me?

ROSE. Just got the word... we're gonna need a good lawyer.... and a *bar tender*. And you're elected.

EVIEL. Me?

ROSE. Lotta laughs and excitement. Whatta ya got to lose? Now, let's eat!

MARIO. *(With authority)* Dodie, you and me, we gotta talk.

(He takes Dodie's arm and they exit to the dining room)

REGINA. *(Takes Eviel's arm, purrs to him)* Tell me, do you really have a black belt?

EVIEL. A brown one, a blue one and a great burgundy lizard-skin my mother gave me for Christmas. Works every time!

REGINA. Oh, God. Brains *and* a sense of humor. Who could ask for anything more? *(Regina takes his arm and they exit)*

ROSE. Say, Joey, did you give me three forks? I like three forks.

JOEY. I always give you three, don't I? Every night by your plate, is there one fork? No. Two forks! NO. Three forks? Surprise! YES! Three freakin' forks, Auntie

Rose. Geez! You and Dad. What do you think I am, anyway?

ROSE. Ah, you're a treasure, Joey. That's what. *The best damned treasure this family ever had.*

(Laughing, they both exit to the dining room)

(Benny, alone on stage, leans against the counter, holds his hands out to the ceiling and besieges Lenora above with a silent plea.)

BLACK OUT

END OF ACT ONE

ACT TWO

Scene I

(Early Sunday afternoon. Benny is in a tizzy, cooking and stirring, peeling and chopping and very plainly, unhappy. Joey is seated in at the table.)

RADIO ANNOUNCER. A Justice Department investigation is under way into the structure of The Secret Family, allegedly headed by the illusive Sarlo Bambino whose minions have controlled the traditional rackets; garbage collecting, loan sharking, jury tampering, the numbers rackets, stolen car rings, and lately, the infiltration of small family-owned businesses, especially Italian restaurants…

BENNY. Turn that darn thing off! I'm getting sicker by the minute listening.

(Joey turns radio off)

How did I get roped into this? I'll do the dinner today and then get rid of them somehow. I don't know how, but if it kills me, I ain't having no restaurant with no Secret Family!

(Rose enters, humming happily. She's wearing a colorful bathrobe and has big curlers in her hair with a big one pointed upwards. She is carrying two baking sheet covered with foil.)

BENNY. *(Points to her head)* What? You need an antenna now to reach La-la-patta- who-who?

ROSE. Benny… as Mamma would say, "Stata zitti!" Shut up.

BENNY. *(Indicates the tray)* What's that you got there?

ROSE. An appetizer. Mamma's recipe and now mine. Stuffed mushrooms.

(She puts them in the oven)

BENNY. Geez! Did the world come to an end and nobody told me? Since when do *you* cook?

(Benny crosses, walking funny, to view the tray)

ROSE. Since when the Mafia comes to dinner.

(She notices his peculiar gait)

Why you walking funny?

BENNY. I'm wearing that truss you bought me. It fits like a diaper and it's pinching the heck outta me. What size did you buy?

ROSE. I don't know. It was discontinued.

BENNY. And I can tell you *why* it's discontinued.

ROSE. Quiet, Benny. I have to get ready. I'll be in the bathroom. Bake those at 350 degrees until they're nice and bubbly on top.

(She calls as she exits)

BENNY. *(Shouts after her)* You don't have to tell me. I'm the real cook in this house.

JOEY. Boy. This is going to more exciting than our usual Sunday dinners.

BENNY. This kind of excitement I didn't ask for and I don't need.

JOEY. Why are you walking funny?

BENNY. I'm wearing that truss Aunt Rose bought. It fits like a diaper. Now start writin'.

JOEY. I *can't*.

BENNY. Whatta ya mean ya can't? You're always writin'. Like the man said, we need Act Two.

JOEY. I can't write when you force me.

BENNY. Why don't you go into your nice, quiet bedroom and write?

JOEY. I can't write unless I'm at the kitchen table… and I gotta feel it and be in the mood.

BENNY. Well, Mr. Dante, just get yourself in the mood, and I want a happy ending. Write!

JOEY. I have to write what I want; not what you want! This is a saga. Someone always dies in a saga.

BENNY. Happy ending! That's it! End of discussion.

(Benny returns to the stove and checks his pots)

Where the heck are your sisters? How long does it take Father Martino to say Sunday mass? Not even the Pope takes this long.

JOEY. They had to pick up the cake at the bakery.

(Angelo saunters in, slickly dressed in a black shark-skin suit, black shirt and white tie… wearing dark glasses. He stands quietly for a second before he begins his work. He bends down… opens lower cabinet door and examines the interior and works his way through the cabinets.)

BENNY. Whoa! Where the heck did you come from? I didn't hear no one knockin'.

ANGELO. Family always comes to the back door. Besides, the front door was locked.

BENNY. I don't remember invitin' *you* into my family. Next time, try ringin' the bell, and if you're here for dinner, it ain't til two.

ANGELO. *(Still bent down, he thrusts one arm up in the air to show his watch)*

I got a watch. I can tell time. Just go on with what you was doing. Ignore me.

(Anglo looks around. He whistles a breathy whistle as he opens whatever cupboards are available and looks inside. He feels around tops of doors, squats and feels underneath the kitchen table. Joey leans over looks under the table, too)

BENNY. This may come as a shock, but you're kinda hard to ignore. Just what the heck do you think you're doin'?

ANGELO. A little preliminary but necessary work.

JOEY. He's checking for "bugs," Pop.

ANGELO. Clever kid. But you gotta go some to outsmart Angelo Pecorino.

JOEY. Wow! Not Angelo, "The Big Cheese," Pecorino?

(Pecorino checks under a chair)

ANGELO. Heard of me, huh?

JOEY. Who hasn't? Is it true that you're manipulating your way up to be the next successor in the power struggle within the Secret Family?

ANGELO. *(Playfully cocks his finger and thumb and aims it at Joey like a gun.)*
That, kid.... POW.... is... a secret.

(On "Pow," JOEY jumps but Benny reacts even more so.)

So, what else ya' hear about me?

JOEY. Only that you're reputed to be the most notorious pit-bull of the enforcers.

ANGELO. *(Speaks to his dead mother)* See dat, Ma? I'm practically a household word.

(Feels under Joey's chair and Joey sticks his legs in the air to accommodate him)

JOEY. You mean like "Ex-Lax"?

ANGELO. Pro-cisely! It takes a lotta smarts and a lotta muscle to make yourself a household word.

(On "muscle," he taps his head)

JOEY. *(Disgusted with his ignorance)* Yeah. *Right!*

(Picks up his pencil and paper)

Say, Mr. Big Cheese, for English class, I have to write about my most memorable character. So far I haven't come up with anyone really special. But, boy... if I write about you... I mean, growing up and everything, and how you achieved your fame... I'll bet I get an A plus. After all, you're *notoriously notable.*

BENNY. Joey, for cryin' out loud! Whatta think you're doin'?

ANGELO. Leave the kid alone. He knows exactly what's he's doin. Notoriously notable, huh? Hoo, boy... I like the sound of dat. Why not? After all, I'm already a legend in the ole' neighborhood.

JOEY. I'll bet you were the toughest kid in your class.

ANGELO. How about the whole *Reform School?*

BENNY. Jo-eey! Will you mind your own bees-wax?!

ANGELO. Look, kid, you and me are gonna get along fine. But I got work to do here first. We'll talk... later, huh? You can do one of them.. one of them..like on t.v... inter... things...

JOEY. Interviews?

ANGELO. One of dem. Do I got stories for you!

JOEY. Great! Give me a for instance.

ANGELO. I don't like to brag, but oh, like for instance the time I.... threw Mr. Coniglio off da Empire State Building.

BENNY. *(Horrified)* For God's sake, why?

ANGELO. He was crampin' my style... so...

(Demonstrates)

...bloop! Man, overboard! A man's gotta protect his reputation... you know.

JOEY. The Empire State Building!? He must have splatted all over the place.

ANGELO. Let's just say....

(Opens up his jacket to reveal seams of the lining...)

.... he kinda came apart at the seams.

(He points down the hallway)

Now, what's down here?

BENNY. Bedrooms.

(Angelo saunters over, feels around doorway, etc., and disappears in the hallway. Benny and Joey stare after him. Suddenly, a loud, blood-curdling scream from the hallway)

Oh... and the bathroom.

ROSE. *(Off)* DID YOU EVER HEAR OF KNOCKING?! YOU PERVERT!

(Angelo rushes back, very shaken by Aunt Rose's outburst.)

JOEY. Find a *bug?*

ANGELO. I didn't do nothin', I *swear.* All I did was walk in by mistake.

MARIO. *(Rushes in)* What's going on in here? Who screamed?

ANGELO. You're hearin' things. Get back out front and wait for the guests.

MARIO. Are you sure? Benny? Joey?

ANGELO. You tellin' me I'm pro-vocker-atin'?

MARIO. *(Backs out to the doorway)* You... lie? No, of course not. Never. I just thought... well, I'd better... get... back...

ANGELO. Yeah... do dat. And don't come in until I tell you.

(Mario begins to exits but Angelo shouts after him.)

Come back in here!.

(Mario re-enters. Angelo shouts at him, again, showing his control)

Get outta here!

(Intimidated, Mario exits)

JOEY. *(Disappointed, writes in his book)* WOW! Mario.... W-I-M-P!

ANGELO. *(Sinister wink)* Wanna get along with the Big Cheese... you gotta learn to take orders.
Hey! I'm gettin' hungry. Like the little girl said, I had only a light breakfast.

(He saunters behind the counter and picks up a roll from a basket)

BENNY. *(Slaps his hand knocking the roll back into the basket)* We didn't say nothin' about servin' no brunch!

ANGELO. Excu-s-e me!

(He lifts a pot lid. Sniffs.)

U-m-m-m. What's this stuff?

BENNY. *(Angrily)* Trippa alla Romana!

ANGELO. Tripe? I hate tripe. And, I don't eat *rabbit*.

BENNY. Who said I was cookin' rabbit? You got two choices; take it or leave it! You eat what I put in front of you.

(Benny grabs the lid from him and replaces it with a clank.)

ANGELO. What are you? My mother? What else you havin'?

BENNY. *(Picks up each pot lid and dish and recites the menu)*
If you have to know… Zuppa Fresco del Mare, Canneloni alla Regina, roast veal stuffed with my own sausage, Chicken Sorentino, baked, stuffed artichokes, with home-made peasant bread…all my own personal recipes.

ANGELO. Dat all?

BENNY. *(Continues reading)* Tongue salad…. Chicken Livers Livornese, Ziti al Forno, pickled eggplant, hot peppers with anchovies, and Spinach and Troofle *frit-ta-TA!*

JOEY. Tell him what's for dessert, Pop.

BENNY. Home-made cannoli. Three kinds!

(Opens refrigerator door and points to desserts)

JOEY. Don't forget the birthday cake.

BENNY. *(Slams refrigerator door)* Okay? You approve now?

ANGELO. I notice you didn't mention no antipasto.

BENNY. *(Lifts a towel over a tray to show him)* With such important company, here's the antipasto.

JOEY. Yeah! Mr. Big Cheese, if you're so important, how come one of your soldiers isn't doing the bull-work?

ANGELO. You want somethin' done right, you do it yourself. Best piece of advice you'll ever get.

(Enter Dodie and Regina. Dodie carries a cake box.)

REGINA. I could have sworn Mario was afraid to come into the house with us.

DODIE. My Mario's not afraid of anything! My Mario is brave and *gauntless*.

(Spots Angelo. Bubbling and bright, they exchange a friendly kiss)

Well, look who's here. If it isn't Lieutenant Angelo. You're early.

ANGELO. Yeah…. I was just…. goin' over the menu with your father here.

DODIE. Oh. Lieutenant, may I *prevent* my sister, REGINA?

ANGELO. Prevent her from what?

REGINA. *(Offers her hand)* Just say how do you do.

ANGELO. How do you do! Hoo-boy! Two beauties from the little chef here? Now that's what I call a real long shot.

DODIE. Look, everyone.

(Dodie opens a corner of the cake box and allows Angelo to peek in.)

That Cousin Theresa, pregnant out-to-here and ankles swollen like watermelons, really outdid herself this time. Isn't it beauty-ful? And she put in three candles… one for the past, present and future.

(Dodie sets the box on the counter)

ANGELO. Well, if that ain't apropose. Past, present and… *(he coughs)*..the future.

ANGELO. Where's the dining room?

REGINA. Through there. Why?

ANGELO. I have to finish. Excuse me. Ladies?

(Salutes them with a grandiose bow as he exits)

REGINA. Finish what? What's he doing, Daddy?

BENNY. Don't ask!

(Aunt Rose enters with an elaborate hair-do and a dressy caftan.)

AUNT ROSE. Where did that *creep* go? Who the heck was he, anyhow? I'll show him a thing or two.

JOEY. I think you already did.

ROSE. That lousy so-and-so not only startled me, but he sent my psychic center into Code Red. Bad vibes, Benny.

Bad vibes! Wait.

(Sniffs the air loudly)

I smell... cheese. Not Asiago. *(Sniff)* Not Parmesan. *(Sniff).* Yes! Pecorino Romano.

JOEY. Auntie Rose, you are fantastic. That's who that was. Angelo Pecorino.

ROSE. Oh, my God... that hardened criminal? But don't worry... I'll soften him up.

BENNY. *(Pleading)* Please, Rose... you'll only make things worse.

ROSE. Oh, all right... all right!

(She addresses Regina)

Say, Regina, I hear you two had a hum-dinger of an evening last night. Lots of action from the Lebanese front with a little Armenian rocket propulsion thrown in...

REGINA. Auntie Rose! You're embarrassing me.

ROSE. Excuse me. What I meant to say was that you charmed the pants off of him.

REGINA. *(Angry)* Dodie, I told you not to tell.

DODIE. I never told a soul... I swear! I didn't do anything.

ROSE. Quit picking on her. It was La-lu-pat-a-la-la.

BENNY. Geez Marie! Not him, again!

ROSE. He only kept me up half the night giving my a blow-by-blow. I think he likes to watch. I'm exhausted. Remind me to take a sleeping pill the minute you leave on the honeymoon.

DODIE. Did you hear that, Daddy? Honeymoon!

BENNY. When are you all gonna stop believin' everything she says! She's nuts!

REGINA. Auntie Rose, I think I actually felt something meaningful... for the first time in my life.

DODIE. Oh, Regina. Do you mean... you have finally found the guy who can plop the cherry on your hot fudge sundae?

REGINA. Maybe *two* cherries!

BENNY. They're talkin' about *fruit* when we may all be history in an hour.

REGINA. It was extraordinary, the feeling… that sensation… a tingling ache right inside… here, and it went a-l-l the way down and wound its way ar-ound to my stomach and ended up in my throat. I could hardly catch my breath.

BENNY. Mr. Fusco, two blocks over, felt that same pain. They said it was angina.

DODIE. *(Crosses to the oven and opens the door)* Wow! What smells so good?

ROSE. *(Very blasé)* Merely the specialty of the house. My appetizer for the Bambino's. Wild Mushrooms.

REGINA. *(Looks in the oven)* Aunt Rose… *you* made these? They look wonderful!

ROSE. Hand-picked and stuffed by me personally.

(Emphatically)

But these are *not* for *you*. **Understand?** They are *only* for the Bambino family. See, they're all going on a short… *vacation*… and I prepared a special treat to give them a little send-off. So… *you* don't eat them, *capeesh*??

DODIE. *(Shrugs)* Sure, Aunt Rose. Whatever.

REGINA. Okay… okay. Whatever you say.

(Benny registers alarm)

ROSE. Now, go get ready and take the prodigy with you.

(To Joey)

You! Change your clothes. You've worn that shirt for three days.

JOEY. Phooey! It's un-American to get clean for dirty crooks. You'll read about this in my documentary and I won't be kind.

REGINA. We're getting wrinkles from worrying. Come on you!

(They exit with Regina tugging at a protesting Joey).

JOEY. And that's exactly how I'm portraying you... ugly and wrinkled, with hooked noses!

(They exit)

BENNY. Rose, I want to talk to you.

ROSE. Not now, Benny... I'm busy. We'll talk later.

(She exits to the dining room. Almost immediately, she screams loudly and rushes back into the kitchen))

BENNY. What's the matter? What's happened in there?

ROSE. *(Startled)* There's a man laying face up underneath the dining room table.

BENNY. Is he dead?

ROSE. I didn't wait to take his pulse.

BENNY. Maybe we should call the police.

ROSE. NO! No police! For God's sake! You want the entire underworld to descend upon us.

(Mario enters and stands at the door)

MARIO. Did I just hear someone mention *police?*

(Angelo enters, brushing himself off and straightening his tie)

ANGELO. *No one* calls the police. Got it!

(To Mario)

You! Get over here!

(Mario complies)

Get outta here!

(As Mario begins to exit, Eviel enters. They face each other and Eviel again affects his silly Karate pose. Mario exits)

ROSE. Eviel... come in. Oh... you look so handsome.

ANGELO. Who's this?

BENNY. This is Eviel Kharren.

ROSE. Our... *bartender.*

BENNY. Eviel, this is... Angelo Pecorino

EVIEL. Wait a minute! You're not *the* ANGELO PECORINO? "The Big Cheese PECORINO?" You're practically a household word.

ANGELO. *(With pride)* Yeah. Like Ex-Lax.

ROSE. *(She pulls Eviel aside. Quietly)* Did you bring what we talked about?

(Eviel nods and pats his shirt pocket)

Good. Now go set up the bar. It's in the dining room.

(Eviel exits)

BENNY. Rose, I need to talk to you.

ROSE. Later. I don't have time right now.

(Checks the oven)

I think you'd better check the place settings on the table out there. We'll talk *later*...

(Benny throws his hand up and exits to the dining room, leaving Rose and Angelo alone)

(Rose checks the mushrooms in the oven)

ANGELO. Hey, lady. Sorry I scared ya before but there's a simple explanation. I... I... had to lie down for a minute in there because I got one of dose bad migration headaches.

ROSE. *(With disdain)* HA!

ANGELO. I don't think we've officially met. I'm Angelo Pecorino. I don't know your name.

ROSE. Good. Let's keep it that way.

ANGELO. How about if I pin one on you?

(He thinks)

How about.... *Sophia Loren?*.

ROSE. *(Begins to soften)* Really. I'm always being taken for her. Rose. Rose Scrivente.

ANGELO. Rose! What a *beauty-ful* name. A rose by any other name... smells as... *good* as what's comin' out of that oven....

ROSE. *(Softening more)* My specialty. Wild Mushrooms. Stuffed 'em myself.

ANGELO. Mushrooms. I knew it! Wow! Boy, that brings me back to when I was a kid.

(Reminiscing, makes an ersatz Sign of the Cross ending it in the air)

My mother… God rest her soul… she used to pick mushrooms.

ROSE. My mother, too! In the old country.

ANGELO. I'd sit at the table and she's say… "Angelo… mangia… mangia.

(He picks up a wooden spoon and slaps at an imaginary child because his mother was angry at him.)

Eat, eat Little Pecker."

Those were the days, huh? Being a kid.

(He looks closely at Rose. He leans towards her.)

Hey… you know, you have beauty-ful eyes. You can tell a lot about a person by looking into their eyes. You married?

ROSE. No.

ANGELO. I can't believe it? Nobody snapped you up?

ROSE. You married?

ANGELO. *(He shrugs)* Me? Nah.

(He's really becoming smitten)

Hey… maybe later… you and I, we could…. we could… you know…

ROSE. What? We could… *what?*

ANGELO. Oh, if only I had met you twenty years ago….

(Mario enters, interrupting and breaking the mood. Rose and Angelo jump apart and resume their previous demeanor)

MARIO. Everything all right in here?

ANGELO. *(Imperious, tough guy again)* Yeah… yeah. Everything's fine. We're just… uh..going over the seating arrangement.

(He removes a seating plan from his inner coat pocket)

ROSE. *(The mood is broken)* So, how many places did we set for? Twelve, or is it fourteen?

ANGELO. Fifteen with the monseigneur from Colombia and the two priests from Argentina.

(He hands her the paper)

Here's the seating arrangement. It's to be *exactly* like this.

(Flirtatiously… softens)

Got it?

ROSE. *(Flirts back, sexily)* Got it!

(Refers to the paper)

Mario, you should be honored. He's got you seated to the right of The Don.

ANGELO. Do you have enough chairs?

ROSE. Oh, we got plenty from the funeral parlor. I'll go check.

(Rose exits to the dining room, but Angelo walks with her, doing a little two-step, flirtatious walk until she is out the kitchen. Rose plays along willingly.)

MARIO. *(To Angelo)* You got me sitting next to The Don? I wasn't gonna eat. I'm supposed to frisk people at the door.

ANGELO. You'll frisk…. then eat! And frisk the monseigneur good. There's no telling what he's got under those skirts.

MARIO. But to sit beside The Don! What do I have to do to deserve such an honor?

ANGELO. *(Crosses downstage, pulls out a huge file and files his nails as he speaks)*

Mario, veni qui.

MARIO. Why are you talkin' in Italian?

ANGELO. Per che questa particolare cosa e molto privato.*

*Pear-kay questa par-tik-o-lar-a causa eh mol-to pri-vah-to.

MARIO. Oh. You don't want anyone to understand our private affairs.

(Looks around)

But there's no one here.

ANGELO. *(Leans in to Mario conspiratorially; looks to see if they are being overheard)( )*

Allora, Mario, sotto la tua sedia*, vicino** il Don… sta uno **revolver.**

MARIO. *(Repeats to him)* You hid a gun under my chair next to The Don.

(Realizes what he said)

YOU HID A GUN UNDER MY CHAIR NEXT TO THE DON!??

(Angelo slaps at him a couple of times.)

ANGELO. *Stoonato!**** Quiet!

MARIO. And what am I supposed to do with this gun that's hidden under my chair next to The Don?

ANGELO. *(Off-handed)* Quando il Don drinks his champagne toast…. Pow. Pow. You shoot him.

MARIO. *(Quaking)* ME?

ANGELO. Pass this loyalty test, you'll be in *all* the way.

MARIO. When I do… this… POW… POW… where will you be?

ANGELO. Right… behind… you.

(Turns him around, roughly shoves him and Angelo exits to the outside)

MARIO. *(To himself after Angelo exits, he whines like a child)*

But I don't wanna shoot The Don!

(Dodie enters, all dolled up for the party, her shoulders exposed)

DODIE. Mario, what are doing here? I thought you needed to be outside *flossing* people

MARIO. Wow, baby! You look sen-sational.

* *SEH-jah*
** *vee-jean'o*
***Stoon-AH-toe

DODIE. Yeah? Well, wait til you see me on our wedding day.

MARIO. Dodie Scrivente, you're like a breath of fresh air.

(He kisses her on the shoulder)

Wow! What smells so good?!

DODIE. Like it? It's my new perfume.

(She throws her head back and strikes a pose)

Trojan Princess!

MARIO. Yeah, but I think it's coming from the oven. What is that?

(He opens the oven door and looks in)

DODIE. It's Aunt Rose's specialty…

MARIO. I didn't know Aunt Rose cooked.

DODIE. This is probably the first time, so that's why it's so special. She said it was an *apple-teaser*… only for the Bambino's. Stuffed mushrooms… but none of us can have any. She might run out of them.

(She mimics Aunt Rose and shakes her finger at him)

"But you can't have any… capeesh?"

(She continues)

See, the Bambino's are going on vacation and she's giving them a little send off. Isn't she thoughtful?

MARIO. *(Suspicious)* Vacation? Vacation…. Honey, I love you, but I gotta get back to work.

(At the door, he turns to her)

You look beautiful.

(He exits. Rose enters with Benny following)

BENNY. *(Desperately)* Rose! I need to talk to you. Right now!

(He walks briskly, but funny)

DODIE. Daddy, why are you walking funny?

BENNY. Don't ask. They need you in the dining room. Go.

(As Dodie exits, he calls after her in disapproval of her scantily clad figure)

Isn't the rest of that dress still hanging in the closet!?

(He turns to Rose)

Rose! I said I need to talk to you.

ROSE. Benny, I don't have time for idle chit-chat. I have work to do.

BENNY. Rose, what kind of mushrooms did you pick, and don't lie to me.

ROSE. Very special ones, Benny, and you know I never lie.

BENNY. *(Almost in tears)* I want to get rid of them, Rose, but not with poison mushrooms!

ROSE. Hey! I may be crazy, but I'm not that crazy. What would we do with a roomful of dead Mafiosi? Stuff 'em, dress 'em in Santa Claus suits and stick 'em in people's chimneys at Christmas? Use your head! Our refrigerator is too small.

BENNY. Where did you get those mushrooms, Rose, and what kind are they?

ROSE. Hold your water! I got them in back of the cemetery. Mamma showed me years ago. Everybody thinks they're poison but they're not. They're delicious. They're tangy at first, and then sweet, but in thirty minutes.... *Woo!* They're also aromatic and woody-flavored.

BENNY. The *heck* with the woody flavor! *What?* In thirty minutes, *WHAT?*

ROSE. Nothing! Everybody gets... *everybody gets...*

BENNY. Will... you spit... it **OUT!!**

ROSE. Let us just say... everyone will experience a... revelation... an Armageddon.

BENNY. *(Screams at her)* What the heck are you talkin' about!

ROSE. There will be an a rebirth... an apocalypse, a battle between good and evil, if you will.

BENNY. What am I? An alien in a foreign country? How

come I don't understand one word comin' outta your mouth?

ROSE. In other words, they're going to "trip!"

BENNY. You mean like trip… over the carpet? Over the stairs? Trip over **what?**

ROSE. *(She shouts)* **Oh, for Petes's sake, Benny. They're going to get…. *stoned!***

BENNY. WHAT? Oh, my God! I'm a dead man.

BLACK OUT

End Scene I

Scene II

(Not even an hour later. The lights come up almost immediately. Before they do, strange noises emanate from the dining room from fifteen men; some boisterous laughter, the sounds of O-o-o-s's, some weeping, and someone singing in operatic-style "Oh, Marie!". A distraught Benny is a nervous wreck, doing general dinner preparation things while literally going around in circles. Joey is standing at the pass-through window, agog with the spectacle. Everybody is singing "Happy Birthday")

JOEY. *(Looking into the dining room)* **Wow!** Guess what the two priests from Argentina are doing?

BENNY. What?

JOEY. The tango.

JOEY. Wow! Guess what the Monseigneur is wearing under his robes?

BENNY. What?

JOEY. Bikini underwear.

BENNY. Will you stop with the wow's already!

JOEY. But Pop, I got Act II, Scene I without even trying! It's a *dream come true.*

BENNY. It's nightmare alley out there, is what it is!

JOEY. Why do you always spoil everything? They're just getting going good. I need this to unblock.

BENNY. Then drink a glass of prune juice.

(Rose enters)

ROSE. If you'll forgive the pun, they're *wild* about my mushrooms! Pecorino must have eaten a dozen all by himself.

BENNY. Oh, no! How many did you prepare?

ROSE. It's a big cemetery, Benny.

(Regina enters with empty tray)

REGINA. Aunt Rose, we need more mushrooms. The Don refuses to eat another mushroom unless *Merry Lynn* sits right beside him and hand-feeds him.

(She takes baking sheet from the oven and removes mushrooms with tongs.)

BENNY. You didn't give any to him! At his age, they might kill him.

ROSE. He swallowed half a dozen before I could stop him.

BENNY. What happens if you eat too many?

ROSE. Well, sometimes you babble; sometimes you barf. But you usually get a bigger, better buzz.

BENNY. Where is that Mario? He got us into this mess, and before this day is over I'm going to make pasta fazool out of him.

JOEY. Forget it, Pop. He's a wimp; probably hiding behind the couch, and not for research, either.

REGINA. He's not hiding. He's arguing with Angelo over Dodie's chair but I don't know why. We got plenty from the funeral parlor.

(Rose suddenly sticks her fingers in both ears and wiggles them back and forth)

ROSE. Oh… oh! Wait a minute. Wait a minute. It's La-lu. Coming through loud and clear.

REGINA. What's he saying, Aunt Rose?

BENNY. *(Screeching)* Are you crazy, Regina. We're in an asylum right now and you're helping the head lunatic.

ROSE. *(Takes one finger out of her ear)* Quiet, Benny… you're interfering with my reception.

(She replaces her fingers, listening intently)

Uh-huh. Uh-*huh*! Uh-huh. Okay… okay. Gotcha!

(Removes her fingers)

Regina, tell Eviel to get in here right away.

(Regina and Joey exit together)

BENNY. Would someone please tell me what's going on around here?

ROSE. Look, Captain Queeg, everything is right on schedule.

(Eviel enters)

EVIEL. I love it! It's an absolute circus out there. I don't know what's in those mushrooms, but they're going like hot cakes. You Italians sure know how to throw a party. You have the Lebanese and the Armenians beat seven-ways-to Sunday!

(A beat)

So… what is it? Regina said you needed me right away.

ROSE. I just received information from an obscure but credible source. I am his vessel in this world.

BENNY. If a vessel is anything like a bucket, I can tell you what it's full of!

(Regina enters)

ROSE. Quiet, Benny! Eviel, you're a contract lawyer, right?

EVIEL. Right.

REGINA. And he's one heck of bartender… let me tell you!

(She growls a throaty growl at Eviel)

I love your timber!

EVIEL. The effect you have on me is illegal!

(He growls back at her… and they both growl at each other.)

BENNY. What? Are we in the freaking Bronx Zoo? Quiet!

ROSE. All right, Eviel, did you bring what I told you?

EVIEL. *(They sit at the table. Eviel removes the contract from his pocket and reads)*

It's right here. "I, Angelo, also known as the Big Cheese Pecorino, as Official Representative of the Sarlo Bambino family, absolve and release the Benjamin Michael Scrivente family from any and all present or future personal and business relations, from the removal of kneecaps…. the *involuntary* removal of kneecaps or any other such body parts, or the introduction of foreign objects, such as bullets of any caliber, knife blades of any length, poisons of any kind….

BENNY. ...or the... garotte. Don't forget the garotte. Please.

ROSE. What else should go in there?

EVIEL. Definitely.... "without reprisal or retribution"....

ROSE. Make it sound good and legal and binding.

EVIEL. It will be legal and binding, all right but only if it's dated and signed by The Big Cheese himself in two different places.

ROSE. Start writing and date it today. Hurry!

(Evie writes with speed)

EVIEL. *(Dates the document)* Dated this day of... da... da sign here in two places.... It's finished!

(Joey enters)

JOEY. *(Very excited)* Hey, Pop! Get this! The.Don.... is *senile.* He thinks DODIE is **Marilyn Monroe!**

(The Don enters through the swinging door, his trousers are off, and he wears an outlandish pair of boxer shorts. His necktie is tied around his head. Black socks are held up by garters... Eyes wide, hands outstretched, he turns around in circles slowly, marveling at the phantom colors in the air.)

THE DON. *(In awe)* Ah-h-h-h! Look-a! Look-a! *Mamma mia!!*

JOEY. It's The Don.

BENNY. *That's* what's been striking terror in the hearts of men? He's a twerp. I've stepped on bugs that were bigger.

THE DON. Ah-h-h! Che bedda colore!

ROSE. What did I tell you? He's seeing colors!

(The Don makes patterns in the air tracing the colors. He becomes more awe-struck with each one.)

THE DON. Rosa!

ROSE. Pink.

THE DON. Porpora!

ROSE. Purple.

THE DON. Arancia!*

*Ah-RANCH-ee-ah

ROSE. Orange.
THE DON. Blu!
ALL. BLUE!

(Dodie enters carrying The Don's trousers.)

DODIE. *(As if scolding a child)* There you are, you sneaky, little Donnie. I fo-u-n-d you. Now it's your turn to look for Merry Lynn! But if you want to play and hide-and-go seek, you have to dress properly. Look at you. You're coming... a-l-l apart.

THE DON. Hoo-hoo-hoo-! Merry... Lynn! La piu *beddissima** movie starr-rra of-a da whole-a world-a!

(They are facing each other. The Don suddenly slumps forward with his nose right in Dodie's bosom)

DODIE. Isn't... he... *adorable?* He thinks I'm you-know-who! Oh, you sweet little thing.

(His arms hang limply as he collapses against her chest, still standing. She staggers back a bit as she tries to hold him up.)

Now, come on, silly. Come up for air.

(She giggles.)

That's what I always say to Mario.

BENNY. Geez! Don't tell me that!

DODIE. *(She pats The Don on the cheek. Sing-song to him.)*
Oh... Mister Donnie, hon-ey. That is not where you're supposed to hi-i-de!

(She pats him on the cheek again)

Yoo-hoo? Mr. Don?

(Alarmed)

Dad-dee.... Is something wrong? He's not moving.

BENNY. *(Crosses to examine him)* Holy bananas! He ain't breathin', either!

DODIE. You mean... he's... *he's.... Oh, no!*

REGINA. Oh, my God!

* *pew bedd-ISS-ima*

DODIE. Someone... *help!*

(Eviel and Benny lift him and place him on the floor.)

REGINA. Oh, no! Daddy! He looks... he looks....

BENNY. *(Extremely alarmed)* Looks it to me! Whatta you think, Rose?

ROSE. I think we all have 20-20.

(There is much noise in this scene)

EVIEL. *(Points to the dining room)* We should notify the Family!

(Dead silence for a second as they all stop to consider and they decide to ignore his advice and the noise and confusion begins anew at the former intensity)

DODIE. *(Tearfully distraught)* Gawd, Regina! I killed him. I didn't mean to. I loved him. All I did was hug him to my bazoons.

REGINA. Don't cry, honey. He died happy and horny.

BENNY. All I was supposed to do was cook a lousy Sunday dinner!

DODIE. *(Takes command)* **Wait!** Stand back. My mind is suddenly clear

BENNY. Whattaya suppose that means, her mind is clear?

JOEY. It means expect the unexpected.

DODIE. The shock left me with a *monetary* mental lapse. *I know PCB.* Mario does it to me.

ROSE. *That's* a new name for it.

BENNY. What the heck is PCB?

DODIE. You know! VCR? RCA?!!! QVC?

ALL. C... P... R!

DODIE. Yeah. That!

BENNY. Well, then, for Pete's sake... don't just stand there. DO IT.

*(**DODIE** rushes to his side, gets on her knees with her back to the audience and begins her ministrations. She pushes on his chest.)*

DODIE. One..two... three.... *(pause)*

ALL. FOUR!

DODIE. I know that! I'm just thinking what comes next. Oh.

(Dodie appears to place her mouth over The Don's and breathes into him several times. After a while, The Don's hand comes up very slowly and firmly grabs one of Dodie's buttocks. Still on her knees, she shoots bolt upright.)

DODIE. Mario! Is that you?

THE DON. Hoo-hoo! Merry Lynn.... I *loff* you! Kees-a me.

DODIE. It's *him*. Look everyone. He's alive! He's alive!

(They help him up, walk him to a counter, prop him against it on the floor)

(Angelo enters backward with his hands raised high. Mario is behind him, holding the gun on him.)

ANGELO. NO! DON'T SHOOT. DON'T SHOOT!

(Everyone ducks and screams shrilly.)

EVIEL. For God's sake, man, don't do it! You'll go to prison.

MARIO. Not with this thing. I emptied it. Someone loaded it with blanks.

(Fires a round into the ceiling)

ANGELO. *(Crying his heart out)* I d-i-i-d-d!

MARIO. You did?! But why?

ANGELO. *(weeping)* I couldn't hurt da Don. If he had a mustache, he'd look just like my mother..

(A beat)

And... I'm scared of guns.

ROSE. *(Grabs pencil and pad and shoves it at Joey)* Quick, Joey. Write this down for posterity.

ANGELO. And I'm scared of all dem guys out there. Dey do b-a-d things, with blood..and everything. Blood makes me *sick*. I just want *out*. *I want my moth... er!* Mamma. Mamma? Where are you? Your little "pecker" needs you-hoo-hoo!

(Angelo wipes his nose on his sleeve.)

JOEY. *(Begins his "professional" interview.)* Here, Mr... *Peckereeno*, have a seat right here, sit back and calm down. We're all family. And, blow your nose, will you?

(Hands him one of Benny's good dish towels. Pecorino blows his nose twice and lays the dishtowel on the table)

Now, sir, rumor has it that you're afraid of guns. Hasn't that made your job a little difficult as an infamous mobster?

ANGELO. No. You let everyone else do the dirty work and you take the credit and hope no ever finds out. O-o-o-h, and I hate the part where dey punch people. Or when dey use one of dem wire..neck-laces! Dat smarts! The eyeballs pop out and dangle like a pair of blood-shot earrings..and the tongue swells up and pertrodes like a Genoa salami!

(Both he and Benny clutch their throats and make choking sounds.)

See... I got this reputation... but it's hard livin' up to it when you're a *cow-ward*.

JOEY. But could a coward throw Mr. Coniglio off the Empire State Building?

EVIEL. *(Horrified)* Good Lord! You threw someone off the Empire State Building?

ANGELO. Oh, somethin' else. I'm a liar, to-o-o. I'm afraid of heights. I get dizzy on a kitchen stool.

(Weeping)

I cut up Mr. Coniglio and flushed him down the toi-hoy-let.

BENNY. Boy. He must have good pipes!

ANGELO. OH! Oh, my God! There he is! Mr. Coniglio! Right there. Bigger than life. Don't you see him? He's right there. Oh, God, I am so sorry. Please forgive me.

(He falls to his knees in supplication to the phantom.)

I miss you. Sleeping without you has never been the same.

(Weeping)

Every night in bed I used to stroke your fuzzy tail... and rub your pot belly and l-o-n-g, pointy ears...

ROSE. Madonna Mia! Listen to the man. In Italian, coniglio means *rabbit!*

JOEY. WOW! So, what you're telling us, Mr. Big Cheese, is that you assassinated a *rabbit?*

(Angelo sobs his assent)

DODIE. *(Screeches at him)* A lit-tle bunny?

ANGELO. It was... stuffed!

REGINA. Like a toy, stuffed?

JOEY. How old were you when you offed this Coniglio?

ANGELO. *(He sobs)* Thirty-two-hoo-hoo-hoo...

(Sound of sirens out front of the house)

BENNY. Oh, my God. What's going on outside?

MARIO. *(In complete charge)* Don't worry. I'll take care of this.

DODIE. *(overcome with emotion)* Oh, isn't he wonderful, Regina? I love that man so much. In the museum of my mind, he is my masterpiece... and he is *hung*.

ROSE. Quick, where's the contract?

(Eviel retrieves it, hands it to Rose. She speaks to Angelo as if to a child.)

Hello, Mr. Angelo. Can you understand what I am saying?

(He moans.)

Good! Now, you don't want to be in business with anyone who knows about the Coniglio caper, do you? So, if you'll sign this little, teensy paper right here, and *here*.... extricating us from the Secret Family... And if a certain Mr. Pecorino violates said contract, we go straight to *Bill O'Reilly*.

PECORINO. *(Crying louder)* Oh..no! *Not* **Bill O' Reilly!!** I'll be a dead man!

(Rose guides his hand in the signing of both places, two big X's.)

(Joey enters in an excited rush)

JOEY. Pop, it's fantastic out front! Your so-called guests are all being shoved into paddy wagons. Some of them are crying and boobing all over the place. I am so psyched!

(He rushes out again)

DODIE. But Daddy. They haven't eaten yet. What'll they have for dinner?

JOEY. Probably bread and water.

BENNY. Wait a minute. Let's not forget these two guys.

(The girls begin to collect The Don)

DODIE. What's a paddy wagon?

REGINA. Oh… just a comfortable, city-owned limousine.

DODIE. Oh, good! In that case, come on, sweetie. You have to go by-by, now. Regina?

(The girls put his trousers on talking to him as if to a child, but the Don pulls his shirt tail out of his fly and waves it at them.)

No… no… Donnie… no, no!

(She zips him up. As Dodie and Regina lead The Don out, he grabs Regina's behind)

REGINA. No… no, Donnie. B-a-a-d boy! Bad boy!

THE DON. *(With hurt feelings)* Me? Bad-da boy??

(He starts to cry)

Oh-ho-ho! Me no bad-da boy!

(Rose exits with Dodie and Regina)

ANGELO. *(Still in his mushroom-induced state)* Hey… I can't leave. I ordered the veal chops.

(Benny and Eviel each take Angelo under the arm and exit with him. All is quiet).

(Mario enters the back door. He looks around, sees he is alone, removes his cell phone and punches some numbers. He turns his back to the swinging door and speaks in a conspiratorial tone. He does not see Joey begin to enter. When he hears Mario, Joey steps back and eavesdrops, out of sight.)

MARIO. Pyramid One... Pyramid One. Do you read me?

(Joey steps back behind the door as he observes through a crack.)

Reporting - Seven-six-niner-niner-five. What the heck came down? I didn't call for back-up. Who sent the wagons?

(A beat)

You gotta be kidding. The Attorney General! Son-of-gun! *What* bugs? I didn't get a chance to plant any bugs. And what confessions? There was so much confusion out there, I didn't hear any confessions. Wait a minute.

(Stoops, looks under the kitchen table, detaches a "bug" and holds it up.)

There's gotta be another under the dining room table, too. Sure! Pecorino planted them. Son-of-a-gun. He was serious about gettin' out after all! Congratulations, Pyramid One. Very good collar. Yeah..checkin' in for re-assignment tomorrow. Over and out.

(Returns phone to pocket. Aside.)

Too bad his Mamma's never gonna know, but that L*ittle Pecker* showed some bravery after all.

(Mario exits.)

JOEY. *(Enters, alone in the kitchen)* Wow! Broadway, here I come! ***I got Act Two!***

(Benny and Rose enter, Rose smiling broadly and doing a little jig.)

BENNY. Hey, Rose. What happened out there? You sure look awfully happy.

ROSE. *(Smugly)* Oh, nothing. It's just that Angelo asked me to write to him.

JOEY. *(Shocked)* In prison?

ROSE. He's really not that bad, you know. He's gettin' out in three to five.

JOEY. How do you know?

(Rose points a finger upwards to La-la)

And since my mushrooms were such a hit, I think I'll send him some biscotti's… as soon as I learn how to make 'em. Who knows? I might just end up working in Benny's tratoria when he opens it in four years.

JOEY. *(Excitedly) Really*, Aunt Rose?

ROSE. Got it from a credible source.

BENNY. When are you gonna stop listening to her… she's nuts! And as for me, I say… thank God that's over.

(He rubs his side, as he limps)

Ow! I feel like I been through a meat grinder.

ROSE. Hey, Benny. You know the bath robe I gave you that you refuse to wear? You'll need it next week after your emergency hernia surgery.

BENNY. I think I figured out what's wrong with you, Rose. You've been eatin' those mushrooms all along!

(Points to Mario)

And YOU! If my daughter didn't love you so much, I'd have half a mind to turn you in but I'd lose the down payment on the wedding reception.

MARIO. Don't worry. I quit that job. First thing Monday, I'm goin' back to fork-liftin'.

BENNY. Smart move, buddy! Nothin' wrong with fork-liftin'. Maybe it ain't what you call an excitin' career, but it's good honest work, and my daughters deserves honest, got it? Then I'll be proud to have you in this family.

(Puts his arm around Joey. He gets choked up)

Proud…. like… like this kid here makes me. I don't always say it… but…

JOEY. You *never* say it.

BENNY. *(Even more tearful)* Well, I'm sayin' it now. Joey...

JOEY. *(Lovingly)* Pop... you don't have to. Why spoil your record?

(Joey hands him the same dish towel that Angelo used to blow his nose)

Here. Blow.

(Benny begins to blow his nose on it... but remembers... and tosses it on the floor)

BENNY. All right! Now, whattya say we eat? I got a ton of gastro-atomic food here goin' to waste.

JOEY. Mario, I would be deeply honored if I could sit next to you. And, I'd like to ask you a few questions.

MARIO. Deeply honored? Sure, kid. Whattya wanna ask?

JOEY. Well, I got this great idea for my next play... and I'm going to a need a technical consultant. See... it's about his guy that no one suspects is an undercover cop, acting as temp, operating heavy duty equipment. I'll tell you all about it at the table.

MARIO. No kiddin'! Now where did you come up with a great plot like that?

JOEY. Oh... imagination and research, but mostly... research.

ROSE. All right, let's go! Regina, we need clean napkins. Eviel, pour the wine. Dodie, toss the salad....

DODIE. *(Playfully pretending to be dumber than she already is)* I can do that. Where shall I toss it?

(She holds the salad bowl out as if to throw it)

Gotcha!

(She laughs at her own joke)

REGINA. *(Lovingly)* Oh, Dodie Just go sit down and look beautiful for Mario.

DODIE. Oh, that I can *really* do!

(Dodie and Mario exit)

BENNY. *(To Rose, he tugs at his truss)* Not to look a gift horse in the mouth, but I have to make an adjustment.

(Benny exits to the bathroom)

EVIEL. *(Takes Regina in his arms and growls. Rose and Joey observe)* My dear, I don't know what it is, but whenever I'm near you, my thoughts become downright *unlawful*. Must we stay for dinner?

REGINA. *(Throaty)* Yeah, but let's skip dessert.

(They growl at each other, smooch and exit to the dining room.)

JOEY. It's kinda nauseating, but that's not a bad line. I might use it in the second act.

ROSE. Forget the second act and check the silverware. Make sure I get three forks. I like three forks.

JOEY. I always give you three, don't I? Every night by your plate, is there one fork? Two forks! NO... darn it.... NO! What do you think I am?

ROSE. Right now? A PAIN IN THE ASS! But you're the best pain in the ass this family will ever have.

(She plants a loud kiss on his cheek The lights come down)

Come on. Let's eat! I'm starved!

(Rose exits. Joey is alone. Benny begins to enter but he sees Joey and he steps back concealing himself)

JOEY. *(Looks up at the ceiling)* Ma?

(A beat)

All right!

(Gives a big "thumbs up" gesture to the ceiling.)

In this family.... I'VE JUST BEEN PROMOTED FROM MEATLOAF TO PRIME RIB!

(Joey laughs joyfully as he exits, still unaware that Benny has concealed himself.. After Joey exits, Benny reaches into the kitchen and turns the out the lights.)

THE END

PROPERTY LIST

FURNITURE LIST
Kitchen table and chairs
Stove
Refrigerator
Sink, cupboards
Waste basked under sink
Telephone
Small radio
Small cabinet with shelves
for dishes

LIGHTING FIXTURES
Light switch on upstage wall
Hanging lamp over table
Ceiling light over stove area

PROPERTY TABLE *(off)*
Benny - apron
Regina - greeting card
Bottle of nail polish
Rose - enema bag
Eviel - brief case
Eviel - binder inside brief case
Eviel - Business cards
Eviel - scrap of paper with address
Eviel - contract form and pen
Small "electronic" bug - Angelo
Mario - cell phone
Mario - Leather jacket
Mario - dark glasses

SET PROPS (Act One)
Note book and pencil on table
Calendar on refrigerator
Pot with lid
Large spoon
Assorted pots, pans
Salt & pepper shakers
Glasses, dishes, silverware
Napkin holder
Small dish containing black olives

SET PROPS (Act Two)
Knife for chopping
Cutting board
Two baking sheets, foil covered
Bread basket with rolls
Cake box
Salad bowl with tight-fitting lid

PERSONAL PROPS
Benny - apron
Dodie and Regina, purses
Dodie - chewing gum
Regina - pink slippers
Regina - nail polish
Rose - enema bag
Eviel - brief case with binder inside
Eviel - business cards
Eviel - scrap of paper with address
Eviel - contract form and pen
Angelo - small "electronic" bug
Angelo - wrist watch
Angelo - dark glasses
Mario - cell phone
Mario - dark glasses

COSTUME PLOT

ACT ONE
Benny - grey trousers of a postal worker
grey shirt, frilly apron
Joey - tan slacks, short sleeved shirt
Dodie - colorful, tight pants outfit
Regina - *(1)* tight dress, high heels
        (2) pink slippers
Aunt Rose - brightly colored caftan
  matching scarf in her hair
Eviel - Kharren - business suit, glasses
Mario - black leather jacket, dark glasses

ACT TWO
Benny - dark trousers, white shirt
white chef's apron
Joey - *(1)* same costume as in Act One\
     (2) new trousers, clean shirt
Angelo - black suit, black shirt, white tie
  dark glasses
Aunt Rose - *(1)* bathrobe, hair in rollers
          (2) dressy, colorful caftan
Dodie - *(1)* Dress, high heels
      (2) Dressy formal dress, low cut
Regina *(1)* Dress, high heels
     (2) Dressy formal party dress
Eviel - tuxedo, or black pants, white shirt
bow tie *(dressed as bar tender)*
Mario - suit, tie
The Don - white shirt, tie wrapped around his head
  no trousers, outlandish underwear,
  black socks held up by garters

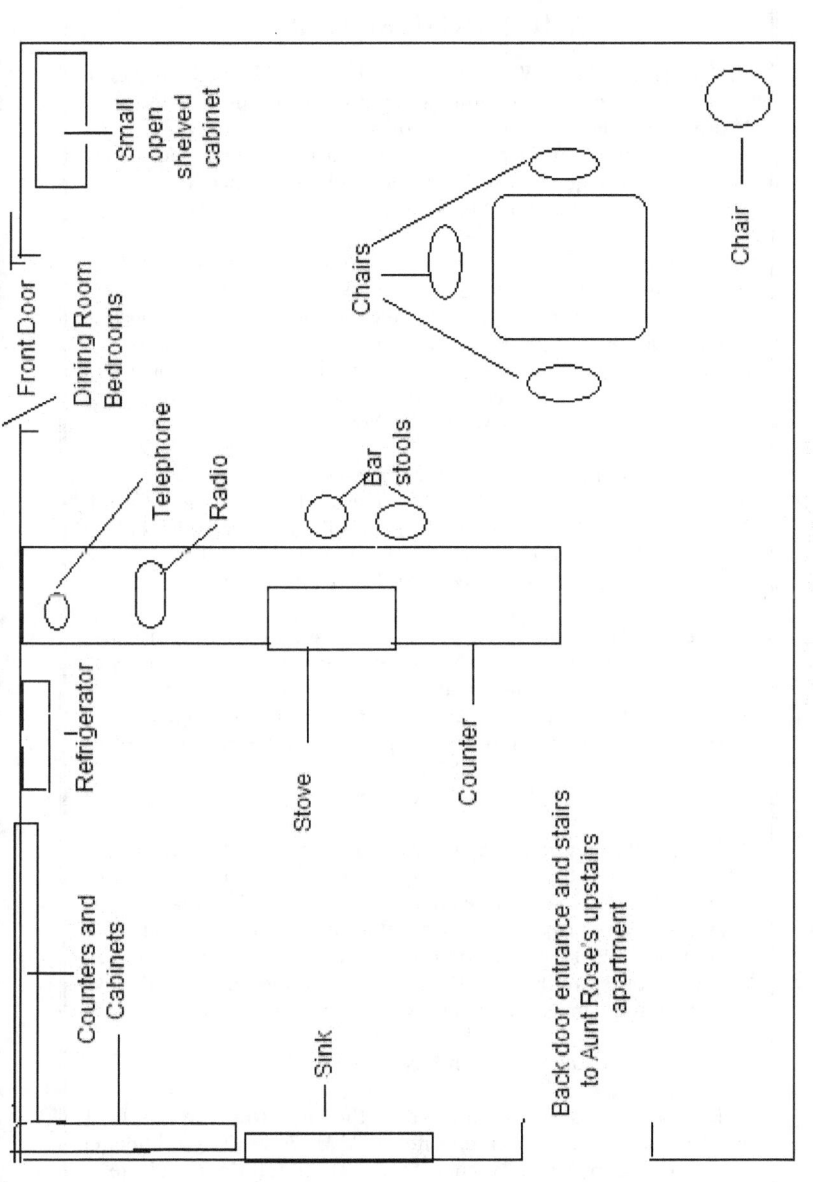

Set for WILD MUSHROOMS

From the Reviews of
WILD MUSHROOMS...

"Don't Trip on Your Way to see *Wild Mushrooms! Wild Mushrooms* is the sweet story of the Scrivente family, an Italian-American group of Bronx residents with a penchant for incorrect word usage, lovingly sarcastic banner and clairvoyance. *Wild Mushrooms* is a complete package certainly well-worth the experience."
- Justin L. Smith, *The Tolucan Times*

"When dining with the Mob, what's on the menu may prove to be the difference between and miss and a hit. *Wild Mushrooms* is a hilarious look at the life in the Bronx and the wisdom of choosing one's friends - and perhaps relatives - most carefully. Aunt Rose manages to save the day and perhaps a few lives with an unorthodox choice of hors d'oeuvres."
Wes Wyse - *NoHo*

"Even as a mentalist and thought-reader, I had no idea the impact that your production, *Wild Mushrooms*, would have on me. I found it to be one of the most delightful and hilarious expositions of a dysfunctional family that I have seen in years."
The Amazing Kreskin, ArcLight Theatre, NYC

"Take one frustrated father who has to postpone his own dreams until he has married off two daughters and sent his son to college, toss in an eccentric clairvoyant relative, mix in some Mafia-like compatriots, measure in a heaping cupful of male marriage-minded candidates and you have the recipe for a hoot and a holler of hilarity."
- *Middletown Press*

"It's a good thing that *Everybody Loves Raymond*, the long-running TV show, has left the air because it could have serious competition from *Wild Mushrooms*. These characters are potential great sitcom figures with appropriate attitudes that should easily cover three or four seasons. However, you don't have to wait for the TV show. You can get the full flavor in the sprightly production that will have you laughing and wondering just how all the antics will resolve themselves."
- Bob and Karen Issacs, *Guilford Courier*

"Benny Scrivente stirs up more than the sauce when he's in the kitchen talking to his deceased wife. *Wild Mushrooms* is a full-fledged "come on-a my house" comedy and it absolutely delighted the audience."
- Joanne Greco Rochman, *Republican-American*

**Also by
Anne Pié...**

At First Sight

Front Street

Please visit our website **samuelfrench.com** for complete descriptions and licensing information

www.ingramcontent.com/pod-product-compliance
Lightning Source LLC
Chambersburg PA
CBHW070647300426
44111CB00013B/2303